The Limelight

The Limelight
A Compendium of Contemporary Columbia Artists
Volume 1

Edited by Cynthia Boiter

Muddy Ford Press
Chapin, South Carolina

THE LIMELIGHT: A COMPENDIUM OF CONTEMPORARY COLUMBIA ARTISTS, VOLUME 1. Copyright 2013 by Cynthia Boiter. All rights reserved. Printed in the United States of America. No part of this book may be used or reproduced in any manner whatsoever without written permission except in the case of brief quotations embodied in critical articles and reviews. For information address Muddy Ford Press, 1009 Muddy Ford Road, Chapin, South Carolina 29036.

FIRST EDITION.

Library of Congress Number: 2013931882

ISBN: 978-0-9838544-4-9

Cover art by Philip Mullen.

Terry—played by Claire Bloom: "I thought you hated the theatre?"

Calvero—played by Charlie Chaplin: "I also hate the sight of blood, but it's in my veins."

From the film The Limelight, *1952*

Created when an oxyhydrogen flame is directed at a cylinder of calcium oxide, known as quicklime, the limelight was first used in London's Covent Garden Theatre in 1837 to illuminate the stars of the stage.

Contents

Gilmer Petroff—*Ballerina in White*
By Aïda Rogers

James Dickey—*In Touch with Darkness*
By Ed Madden

Chris Potter—*Saxophone Colossus*
By Michael Miller

Blue Sky—*Public Artist*
By Cynthia Boiter

Pat Conroy—*How I Stalked My Prince of Tides*
By Janna McMahan

James Busby—*Layers of Talent*
By Jeffrey Day

Marjory Wentworth—*Laureate*
By Kristine Hartvigsen

Danielle Howle—*Musical Light*
By Kyle Petersen

Kay and Jim Thigpen—*Theatre Heritage*
By August Krickel

Nikky Finney—*Poet of Action*
By Colena Corbett

Stephen Chesley—*Artist and Mentor*
By Susan Lenz

Philip Mullen—*Dialogue Artist*
By Cassie Premo Steele

Robert Richmond—*Bravery*
By Chad Henderson

Terrance Hayes—*Punches in the Dark*
By Ray McManus

Stacey Calvert—*Reluctant Teacher*
By Bonnie Boiter-Jolley

Vicky Saye Henderson—*Leading Lady*
By Robbie Robertson

Robert Lamb—*Courage*
By James D. McCallister

Greg Leevy—*The Youngest and the Sweetest*
By Alex Smith

Preface

Humans touch one another's lives in many ways, from acts of kindness to acts of desperation. But when artists touch each other—when they move one another even slightly toward creation—something bordering on the miraculous happens. Inspiration. The exponential power of inspiration cannot be measured in joules or dollars or meters; it cannot be represented on a graph or a pie chart. It can't always even be traced back to its origin. And it is often from the serendipitous that inspiration comes; a slice of conversation, musical notes jumbled in the wind, a movement, a reflection in the water.

When artists—visual, performing, or written word—interact with one another as the artists in this compendium have, both writers and subjects, whether they intend to or not, they influence each other.

In his essay on first reading the work of fellow poet Terrance Hayes, Ray McManus writes of, "Each poem telling me something I should have already known, teaching me something I thought I already knew. I wanted to kick his ass."

Chad Henderson, an already accomplished theatre director in his twenties writes of earlier work as an actor under the director Robert Richmond in the play *As You Like It,* and the way that one specific week of rehearsal proved pivotal in his future work as a professional director. "I owe a lot of my bravery and success to his tutelage—he's made me into a risk taker and he's led me to trust myself. He's showed me the way to impart the same to my casts."

Screenwriter Robbie Robertson confesses that watching local actress Vicky Saye Henderson perform on a Columbia stage resulted in a full paradigm shift in his approach to and reception of local and regional theatre.

Columbia, South Carolina boasts artists of all genres with stories to tell. Some artists, like Henderson, are just beginning their careers. Others, like visual artists Blue Sky and Philip Mullen, or theatre trail-blazers Kay and Jim Thigpen, have careers they could rest their laurels upon, if they chose to do so, though few have. And sadly, a few have left their legacies and moved on, leaving others to analyze or honor them as actor Alex Smith does so well of Greg Leevy, and writer and editor Aïda Rogers does of the late muralist Gilmer Petroff.

Certainly, one book does little toward illuminating the multiplicity of artists and relationships and chance encounters that have resulted in the dynamic arts culture this capital city enjoys. That is why this collection is just the first volume in an ongoing and annual compendium that will continue to honor the creators of this arts culture and be written by its equally creative constituents.

The limelight glows brightly in Columbia, South Carolina, and it casts a long and lasting shadow.

—Cynthia Boiter

Gilmer Petroff

Ballerina in White

By Aïda Rogers

There she is. Not Miss America, but to me a creature much more captivating. Showy tears are not for her, nor a glittery stagger down a pageant runway. The Ballerina in White has discipline. Fortitude. The breeding not to emote in public.

And that's how she's been since 1952, when she and her accompanying cast of figures were introduced on the street level of Tapp's Department Store. Artist Gil Petroff conceived and designed the 42-foot-long mural in which she appears—forever aloof, forever aloft. For sixty years she's stayed true to her training, focused on the faraway and not the shoppers as they entered and exited the elevators beneath her.

I'm not sure how long I've focused on her. She was probably fifteen or twenty years into her life's work when I first saw her. One of four children of a mother who loved to shop on Main Street—back when Main Street throbbed with department stores—I always looked up for her when we went into Tapp's. Checking in, kind of, just to make sure she was there. And she was. Oblivious to me, I was enchanted by her.

I was less enchanted by her landscape. I didn't care about the buildings or the trees, or the other people—they were doing dumb stuff like playing sports. But the Ballerina, in her shockingly short white tutu, was doing what I and so many children did in their dreams. She was *flying*. For a girl whose fervent wish was to be a trapeze artist, she was the closest thing to a role model I had.

Though I faithfully practiced my trapeze routines on the backyard swing set, no circus came to take me away. Nor did any mysteries arrive for me to solve, once I opted for a Nancy Drew career. But in life's long and circular way, a mystery was delivered with this writing assignment. Who was Gil Petroff? And who is the Ballerina in White?

I can only guess at the second, but I've got some firm ideas about the first. Gil Petroff was more than a skilled painter and whiz at architectural drawings, which is how he made his living, it seems. Gil Petroff was one of Columbia's truly great guys. In my search for those who knew him—he died in 1990 at age 77—I heard nothing but excitement and pleasure in the voices of the people I called.

"Good for you!" Candy Waites's voice rings out when I tell her I'm writing about Petroff and his artistic influence on Columbia. Candy is the daughter of the late Edmund and Dorothy Candy Yaghjian, famed Columbia artists who came here from New York in 1945. Gil Petroff and his wife Peggy were family friends. In particular, Dorothy Yaghjian and Gil Petroff were close because they both worked in watercolors. "He really played the part," Candy remembers. To her,

Petroff was a "Santa Claus" kind of person, with his hats, and goatee or beard.

Laura Spong, in her eighties now, says Petroff gave her confidence. She was married with six children in the 1950s when she began art classes at the Columbia Museum of Art's Richland Art School. Classes were, understandably, an "off and on" thing. Petroff was her first teacher. "I loved him," she says. "He was so nice, so kind, so low-key. Plus he was a real fine artist himself. I've always regretted not having a piece of his."

It was Petroff who encouraged her to join the Columbia Artists' Guild, and to experiment with lacquer on Masonite, then in vogue, she recalls. Now an acclaimed painter of abstract expressionist works, Laura thinks her teacher has been forgotten. "I don't think he ever got the recognition he should have gotten," she says. "I would say he was probably not a marketer."

She pauses. On the phone, I hear her smile. "I'm so glad you're doing this."

I'm glad I'm doing this too. I can park myself in one of my favorite places, the South Caroliniana Library, to investigate my subject. Gil Petroff's papers are here, and I'm ready to pounce. A tidy carton of twenty file folders provide clues to his life and photocopies of his work from 1937 through 1991. Assorted newspaper and magazine articles offer details about his history and personality. And, I'm confounded to learn, more mysteries arise.

Here are the basics: Gilmer Petroff was born March 20, 1913, in Saranac Lake, New York. His father was a Russia-born bacteriologist at the Trudeau Sanitarium, a noted tuberculosis clinic in that town. His mother was from Toccoa, Georgia, one of his ties to the South. He studied art and architecture at Yale, and art at the University of Wisconsin and Cape Cod School of Art. He and Peggy, an England-born artist, met during World War II in New York City while working for the same ship designer. They came to South Carolina in 1947 when Gil accepted a job teaching art and architecture at Clemson College. They had three children.

In 1950 the Petroffs moved to Columbia. Gil worked for the now-defunct architectural firm of Lyles, Bissett, Carlisle, & Wolfe and then for Stanley Smith & Sons. From the files, it looks like he drew an endless parade of buildings—from hotels in Myrtle Beach, banks in Columbia and Greenville, and even, God bless him, Pedro's sombrero-shaped water tower at South of the Border.

He also taught at the Richland Art School, which operated through the Columbia Museum of Art. His friendship with the late Dr. John Richard Craft, director of the CMA and a fellow Yale man, was another Columbia draw. Petroff was listed in *Who's Who in American Art* seven times between 1947 and 1976, and his paintings are in collections at the High Museum of Art in Atlanta, the

O'Hara collection in Washington, DC, and in Saranac Lake. In South Carolina, the art museums in Charleston, Columbia, and Florence collected his work, as well as the State Museum. He also has a piece in the state's art collection.

Those are the facts. Now for the fun. Petroff, whose philosophy was "art is for fun," had his share. In 1937 he "motored thru Mexico," according to the *San Diego Sun*, which covered his one-man show there. Here, he belonged to a group of artists called "The Carolina Five." Their names—Armando Del Cimmuto, Eugene Massin, William Halsey, Edmund Yaghjian—gives the impression mid-20th century Columbia was a hotbed of beret-wearing bohemians.

Near the end of his life, he entered the First International Outhouse Competition. Based on a 1983 letter of congratulations, he must have won or placed. (No drawing of his outhouse was in the files, though the application was.) The files, though, make one thing clear: Gil Petroff could do it all and he did. Photocopies of his Christmas cards, calendars, magazine covers, war bond posters—even a 1955 metal sign of children in silhouette for Bradley Elementary School—prove the point.

That sign still exists, though it had been removed in 2001 for the school's renovation. It was in storage until I called. Dr. Erica Fields, Bradley's principal, didn't know its history or who created it, and a phone call to the Richland District One office revealed that if records were kept, they weren't there. Missing too are the iron posts and chains that fixed the sign to the ground. But the good news is that sign itself remains, heavy in weight and playful in spirit. "It's so cute," Dr. Fields said. "We're really fortunate it's still here; during construction anything can happen."

Though he worked in oils and lacquers, illustrated, taught, and made models, watercolors were Petroff's preference. They "race across the paper with liquid swiftness," wrote Edward Alden Jewell, art critic for *The New York Times*.

The scenes in the Tapp's mural do race across the wall. It starts with a farmer following his plow and ends with several churches, people descending their steps. In between are textile mills with their smokestacks, farm animals, South Carolina's statehouse, and people at play. A golfer prepares to swing, a tennis player reaches for the ball, and a football player—a red 37 on his jersey—dives on the field. It can't be coincidence that football star Steve Wadniak, who died in a car accident in 1951, wore Number 37 for USC.

The Ballerina in White floats above them, and below at the bottom right Gil Petroff painted his name and "1952" in block letters. It was unveiled in October of that year to celebrate Tapp's expansion and renovation. Semi-abstract and nearly seven feet high, it was painted by Petroff and three assistants—John Rast, Larry Scott, and David Van Hook. They used lacquer, a substance known for its permanence, on canvas woven specially for the mural by a Columbia textile mill.

A photo caption in *The State* paper says the mural's mission was to show "all phases of community life" in South Carolina. John Richard Craft, the Columbia Museum of Art's director, declared it "one of the handsomest examples of mural painting I've seen anywhere."

And this is where the mysteries present themselves. Gil Petroff had done large-scale murals before—in Glendale, California, and in Staten Island, New York, where he had his own art school. In South Carolina, he'd designed two other, similarly expansive murals—in 1951 for Clemson House on the campus where he most recently taught, and in 1953 for the South Carolina Department of Highways, as SCDOT then was called. The Clemson mural—40 feet long, 7 feet high and billed as the largest painting in the state—depicted a cadet's four-year career at the college. The highway department mural was 35 feet long, 5 feet tall, and covered 200 square feet. It was the "only original mural in a state-owned office building in South Carolina," *The Columbia Record* reported.

Wanting to see more work by a man I was coming to like just by the files I was studying, I figured I'd best take a look at those.

Except I couldn't. They were gone. The Clemson mural, which puzzled and delighted diners when Clemson House housed a restaurant, had been "covered or destroyed during a renovation, probably in the 1960s or early '70s," I learned from Susan Hiott, curator of exhibits at Clemson University Libraries. She'd researched it herself, and though I checked with four other sources, I could learn nothing more. Fortunately, she had copies of an article about the mural and a photo.

No such luck with the highway department. After treks to the current office on Park Street and the former office on the statehouse grounds, several phone calls and emails, I concluded this mural is history too. Margaret Cheek, who worked in both offices, confirmed it. "I couldn't believe they were doing it," she said, remembering when the mural was destroyed. Maybe there was no alternative, she allowed. It was painted on plaster-like walls, she said, perhaps impossible to save when a building is gutted. "I thought it was beautiful," she said, describing a scene with lots of gray roads with "splashes of color."

At Historic Columbia Foundation, John Sherrer shrugs. "It's South Carolina," he says. "It's Columbia." He's the HCF's director of cultural resources; to him, the lost Petroff murals are similar to the grand stage curtains at the now-gone Columbia Opera House. They featured a scene of the Millwood ruins. Nobody knows where they are.

Sherrer is in his early forties—too young to remember the Clemson or SCDOT murals. But he knows the Tapp's mural. "It'd be a travesty for something like that to get lost," he says.

Meanwhile, I learn about a cartoon Petroff drew on a wall of Belk's tearoom. The tearoom opened in 1960. I don't remember the tearoom, but I do remember Belk's. It's gone. The Columbia Museum of Art is close to where it stood. Petroff was a CMA trustee.

———

Maybe I shouldn't be horrified these murals are gone. Maybe the artist himself wouldn't really care.

"It's a shame, but time marches on," says Bobby Lyles, an architect whose father was a partner in the Lyles, Bissett, Carlisle & Wolfe architectural firm that hired Petroff.

I've called Mr. Lyles because I've heard Petroff painted yet another mural that was covered, in the old LBC&W office on Gervais and Barnwell streets, recently vacated by the SC Arts Commission. He confirms that fact, and describes the mural as "shapes." He points me to Petroff's tile mosaic on USC's Byrnes building, on the corner of Sumter and College streets. Lyles was 14 when he helped Petroff build it, he says. I tell him I've examined that mural. I don't tell him I went inside and talked to a lady who works there, who told me nobody asks about it. I don't tell him I'm gratified to read Jeffrey Day's blog decrying the newspaper racks that obscure it.

Like everybody else, Bobby Lyles liked Gil Petroff. And he admired his talent. "It didn't take him time to do anything; he just whipped it out." Lyles had one of his paintings, of shrimp boats, that he gave to his son.

Petroff even helped him with his campaign for mayor of Hand Junior High. His cartoon of Lyles included this slogan: "If you want smiles, vote for Lyles." Mr. Lyles remembers posting the artwork around the school, and that he didn't win.

Did Petroff win? If two of his big murals in the state are gone, and the Tapp's mural is somewhat hidden by a room built when the building was renovated several years ago, it'd be easy to say he didn't. At least the public didn't if his work is in private hands.

There is one exception. At St. Michael and All Angels' Episcopal Church, which he and Peggy helped start, you can see many of his pieces. In the chapel is the portable altar he built, portable so it could be stowed when the church was young and meeting in Satchel Ford Elementary. A cross hangs suspended from the ceiling; Petroff built it with Rev. Jed Sturtevant.

In the sanctuary is the long, slim cross he made from an old fence he found behind the Columbia Museum of Art when it was on Senate Street. The pulpit, lectern, and altar also are his, as is the tile mosaic just outside the sanctuary door. In fact, the sanctuary is his too.

"When it came time for a real church, Dad, with his usual pragmatic approach to architecture, designed one of the prettiest structures you can imagine from components normally used for commercial buildings," Walker Petroff emails me. He is Gil and Peggy's oldest son, an engineer with his own company in Beaufort.

Father Paul Stricklin says the sanctuary was basically a Butler building. I tell him I think this is the only place where the public can see more than one piece of Gil Petroff's work. He responds in a way I think Petroff would like. "Tell 'em it's fifty dollars – sixty if they want me."

———

It's been awhile since anybody asked Walker Petroff about his father, but it still happens. "The ladies in his art classes adored him," he wrote me. "People still come up to us and ask, 'Are you any relation to Gil Petroff?' And they tell some story about him or talk about a painting they have and how much they love it."

Once he put a naked mannequin in the front seat of his VW and drove down Gervais Street, Walker relays, "which got a good bit of attention from other drivers. Dad had a great sense of humor." He also "was generous to a fault and would give you the shirt off his back. Mother and I constantly fussed at him for not charging enough for his work."

And the work is magnificent, Walker believes. "We think he is the foremost watercolorist in South Carolina and maybe one of the finest in the country," he wrote. "I have never seen anyone who could create a sky with realistic simplicity like Dad."

Gil Petroff would be 100 years old this year.

I've never seen one of Gil Petroff's watercolor skies. Right now I'm admiring his lacquer skies in the Tapp's mural. Tapp's is an art center now, home to area artists and events that can be edgy. During one of Columbia's First Thursday festivals, the local circus Alternacirque performed, including a trapeze artist. I think Petroff might have liked that, and that his mural still races across the wall, even though I never could find out who actually owns it and what its future might be.

I can only be grateful that someone has brought a big ladder for me to stand on, so I can study the mural more closely. I see the Ballerina in White has blue eyes and a red mouth, and that she's much thinner than my childhood eyes remember. I wonder if she's supposed to be Margot Fonteyn, the British ballerina of that era. Pictures of her in *Swan Lake* show her in a short white tutu. She flew, too.

When I get off the ladder, I stand back and look at the mural from a distance. And I just can't help it—my head moves right, my eyes move up. I focus on the Ballerina in White. As it was, I guess shall ever be. I can't take my eyes away.

James Dickey

In Touch with Darkness

By Ed Madden

This essay is not an act of revenge.

"If you come on to any of my students, I'm going to come to your office and personally break your fucking neck."

Ten students had signed up for what they thought would be James Dickey's last class, Verse Composition, the deathbed sessions. When he was hospitalized soon after classes began, the department chair, Robert Newman, asked me to teach his class for week—then for a week with the possibility of taking over for the semester if Dickey were unable to return to the class. He suggested I call Dickey in the hospital that afternoon, January 17, to check in with him about the class.

Of course, I had heard the rumors about Dickey's unwelcome comments to (and unwelcome touching of) female students—tolerated, I supposed, because he was our own Great Man at USC, the Strom Thurmond of the literary cosmos. It had become part of his persona. I would later wonder if his threat was just a projection, his fear that I would act like him?

A recently hired assistant professor, I had had little interaction before with Dickey. The first time I remember meeting him was at a department party at the Faculty House, circa 1994, back when the Faculty House was a private club for faculty, filled with (mostly) white patrons and (mostly) African-American staff. Dickey stood to meet the new faculty as we were ushered forward. His jacket, we were told, was a gift from Burt Reynolds. Dickey ignored me and the other men, turning to our new female colleague and feebly twirling her around so that he could "get a better look."

"Or if you teach any homosexual poets, I'm going to come to your office and personally break your fucking neck."

The class would focus on student work, I assured him. It was a poetry workshop. And I was thinking: where is this anger coming from? In Henry Hart's biography, *James Dickey: The World as a Lie* (2000), Hart says that in these last days Dickey found it galling that someone was taking his place in the classroom, so he lashed out at me. Hart's biography also makes it clear that behind Dickey's drunken womanizing persona lay a deep fascination with homosexuality—and likely anxieties about his own ambiguous sexual impulses.

Let me admit: I was intimidated by Dickey. Otherwise it wouldn't have taken a couple of hours for the obvious reply to his comment about "homosexual poets" to hit me: Walt Whitman, W.H. Auden, Elizabeth Bishop, Hart Crane, Robert Duncan, Allen Ginsberg, Thom Gunn, Gerard Manly Hopkins, A.E. Houseman, Langston Hughes, James Merrill, Frank O'Hara, the great war poet Wilfred Owen, Adrienne Rich, (and let's throw in T.S. Eliot, too, just for fun), not to mention Dickey's own friend, Richard Howard.

In the fall of 1995, I had been attacked by a little conservative newspaper on campus for, they said, throwing out the traditional canon to teach "modern homosexual literature" by writers "such as Oscar Wilde." It would have been laughable, maybe, if it hadn't been only my third semester, and if it hadn't been distributed in every student mailbox on campus, and if it hadn't ended with a call to those who weren't happy about my teaching at USC to call me or to contact me, both home phone and home address helpfully provided at the end of the article. I was untenured and unsure of the culture. Though I lived only three blocks from campus, I stopped walking to work. I got an unlisted number and an attorney.

And here I was, barely a year later, talking to a man whose work I admired, who was attacking me in almost the same terms as that conservative student rag.

"And if you've got an ax to grind in the class—particularly that ax—I'm going to come to your office and personally break your fucking neck."

I fumbled through a response about how I didn't have any ax to grind and hung up the phone, stunned by Dickey's three-fold threat. I immediately called the associate chair (I couldn't reach the chair) and told her what had happened. I went to a junior faculty happy hour, still shaken, and told my colleagues. I emailed a close friend, an email I still have. Though my chair had originally suggested I should visit Dickey in the hospital to update him on the class, when he called me later that evening, he said I didn't have to interact with Dickey again unless he was also present.

That was Friday. Dickey died on Sunday evening, January 19, 1997. I heard the news of his death on NPR the next morning, as I sat at the breakfast table with my partner. The semester stretched before me, a graduate writing workshop part of it. I had some very difficult shoes to fill.

Dickey started teaching at the University of South Carolina in the spring of 1969. He had been a military man (in both World War II and the Korean War), an ad man (in New York and Atlanta), and a college English teacher. From 1966 to 1968, just before his move to South Carolina, he had served as Poetry Consultant to the Library of Congress (a position that would later become Poet Laureate).

"So now, as far as I knew," Dickey writes in *Night Hurdling* (1983), a collection of essays, "South Carolina was soybeans, illiteracy, and maybe even pellagra and hookworm, and my chief mental image of it was of a dilapidated outhouse and a rusty '34 Ford with a number 13 painted on it, both covered by kudzu." It's like a scene from a bad movie (or *Deliverance*) or maybe a memory from the brief period Dickey played football at Clemson, before leaving school to join the Army

Air Corps during the Second World War. "Why should I become part of such an environment?"

Dickey says USC president Tom Jones "looked at me with sincere friendliness and said, If you like two things, you would like to live in South Carolina. What two things? I asked suspiciously. Flowers and birds, he replied. Talk on, I said."

Flowers and birds? However much this anecdote—like so many Dickey told—has been embellished, I like to think it's true. As I look up from my laptop, I can see the dogwood that fills my study window every spring with bloom, and the crepe myrtle just beyond, blooming now in this summer's wicked heat. Every afternoon a hummingbird whirs among the zinnias and the canna lilies. But I know that's not the world of Dickey. The natural world of Dickey's writing is not flowers and birds, its snakes and sharks and buggering hillbillies, predatory violence and predatory sex, the elemental and brutal, blood and claw. Under every rock, a rattlesnake.

In Dickey's best poems, he seems to be in touch with some kind of wild darkness, literal and metaphorical. I think about that amazing poem, "The Shark's Parlor," which USC's MFA students have taken on as the name for their monthly readings. In it, an enormous hammerhead shark is baited with buckets of entrails and blood and hooked with a run-over pup by two boys drunk on the "first brassy taste of beer." With the help of other men, they drag the shark out of the sea, dragging it by accident all the way into a beach house, where it thrashes the place to pieces, "throwing pints of blood over everything we owned."

It's the id in the parlor. Among the items destroyed are movie magazines drenched with blood, and the boy's buck-toothed photo—suggesting a darkness belied by Hollywood fictions, suggesting that what you drag up can destroy you, or at least the earlier versions of who you are. The boy-turned-man buys the house, a mark of shark's blood on the wall, "black with time." "It can be touched," he says, only when he has drunk enough.

―

From Hart's biography: Dickey tells a friend, "We hear all this about everybody having gay impulses. I just don't. I can't think about it without a sense of revulsion." Hart adds, "What revolted him when sober, however, had often titillated him when drunk."

―

Although I hadn't read *Deliverance* before I arrived at USC in 1994, I did soon after. I remember thinking immediately that it was like Joseph Conrad's *Heart of Darkness*, adapted for 1970s America. For the frightening black woman at the heart of Conrad's dark jungle, Dickey puts a buggering hillbilly in the dark rural heart of the Deep South, as if to say that the deepest fears of American culture are not race and gender but sexuality and class difference—things we *don't* talk about, or *can't* talk about without euphemism, misrepresentation, or denial (as this year's GOP convention made all too clear).

The film's male rape scene has been reduced in our pop culture lexicon to a joke, with the memorable punch line, "squeal like a pig," but throughout the novel it seems clear that Dickey, though his protagonist Ed, is thinking carefully about what homo sex is and what it means. (Yes, I'm very aware of the strange coincidence of the name, Ed.) After Ed murders one of the rapists, he thinks, "If Lewis had not shot his companion, he and I would have made a kind of love, painful and terrifying to me, in some dreadful way pleasurable to him, but we would have been together in the flesh, there on the floor of the woods, and it was strange to think of it." It's a strange passage, and a strange way to reimagine male rape, but of a piece with the novel's insistent attempts to think about what it *means*.

What are we capable of? There's a thin line between savagery and civilization in this novel, a theme that's suggested earlier, the night before the rape, in a scene that quietly and deeply moves me, filled as it is with a sense of connection with the wildness of nature, not quite or not yet the same as the darkness inside us. "Something hit the top of the tent," writes Dickey. An owl. Ed reaches up to touch the owl's claws, which puncture the tent's thin fabric. "All night the owl kept coming back to hunt from the top of the tent." As the owl hunts the woods, Ed dreams himself hunting with it. And each time it returns to the tent, he reaches up to touch the claws.

The thin membrane of the tent separates him from the wild, but it pushes through. Ed wants to touch it, to be in touch with it. To be in touch with some wildness, some darkness.

———

As a poet, I learn from reading Dickey. Over and over in his poems, there are images that strike me with their surprising accuracy—like the sea in "At Darien Bridge," that "used to look / As if many convicts had built it." There are lines that stick with me, like "Wild to be wreckage forever" at the end of the oft-anthologized and very teachable "Cherrylog Road." Or the wicked ending of "Adultery": "Guilt is magical."

I love the way the flat wildness of his earlier poems can give way to hallucinatory intensities, to madness and mythopoesis, to thickness of sound and sense. Of course there are some poems that don't move me, like the famous long poem "Falling," where Dickey took a kernel of story—the real tragedy of a stewardess being sucked out of an airplane—and inflated it into an overwrought myth, imagining the woman in a free-fall striptease. Taking off her clothes, Dickey turns her into some kind of fertility goddess, with maybe a bit of Oz thrown in (her clothes coming down "all over Kansas"). I can't separate the clunky sexism from the strained symbolism. But then "The Sheep Child," a poem perhaps equally risible in its sexism but one that gives me chills, a poem that can lift a dirty joke about farmboys fucking sheep into myth itself, granting the supposed child a voice: "I saw for a blazing moment / The great grassy world from both sides."

I love the poem "Venom," which transforms a real Florida snake-handler into something godlike. Because of his built-up immunity to snake venom, he repeatedly donated blood to snakebite victims. He lies down "with him the snake has entered," his blood flowing through both their veins. "They will clasp arms and double-dream / Of the snake." I adore the father-son poem "The Magus," in which a new father is like a wise man at Christ's birth. I love that in books of poetry filled with darkness, light is the name for how we connect with one another, for what we can do, for the things we *need* to say. The snake-handler "shimmers / with healing." The young father "is shining to tell you" that his son "is no more than a child," but no less transcendent for that.

All these transformations—humans that become godlike, gods that are mere men.

From Hart's biography: "After one of his groggy lunches in the late 1950s, Dickey picked up a handsome young boy, took him to his office at McCann-Erickson, and closed the door. A startled [colleague] happened to walk in on them. Dickey quickly explained: 'I'm going to teach this boy how to write poetry.'"

By the time I arrived at USC, Dickey was in ill health. I never had a chance to sit in on one of Dickey's classes. I was never included in one of the regular "power lunches" he had with friends at the faculty club, to which selected guests were invited. We never chatted at the mailboxes about what we were reading, or walked across campus together as he waxed on about the poet's mission. I don't remember ever hearing him read.

The only exchange I had with him was a verbal assault from a dying man, a homophobic lashing out that left me shaken and angry.

This essay is not an act of revenge.

I think it may be a statement of regret.

When Dickey taught the graduate poetry workshop at USC, he taught it as a two-semester course, the first a series of exercises in formal verse (ballads, sestinas, sonnets, villanelles), the second semester focusing on poems based on dreams, fantasies, lies.

In my writing classes, I sometimes give an assignment: write a poem or an essay as an act of revenge. Such writing may not see print, but the students seem energized to tap into that darkness, that wild and visceral well of suppressed emotion that can gush up, surprisingly. Later, I give them a related but perhaps more difficult assignment: write a poem as an act of forgiveness.

I like to think James Dickey would approve.

Notes

Dickey, James. *Deliverance.* 1970. New York: Dell, 1994.

----. *The Whole Motion: Collected Poems, 1945-1992.* Hanover and London: Wesleyan UP, 1992.

Chris Potter

Saxophone Colossus

By Michael Miller

It was a Tuesday night in the spring of 1988, and I decided to head down to Pug's in Five Points for the weekly jazz session. Columbia had a lively little jazz scene at the time, and a core group of stellar musicians not only jammed regularly at Pug's but also invited guest players to sit in.

I settled in at the bar as guitarist Terry Rosen played a solo over the rhythms of drummer Ted Linder and bassist Jon Schwabe. I noticed trumpeter Johnny Helms nodding his approval and waiting for the cue to join in. Then I saw a kid who looked no more than 15 or 16 years old standing next to Schwabe, holding a tenor saxophone, and gazing at the floor as he concentrated on Rosen's solo.

"Who's that kid, and how did he get in here?" I asked the bartender.

"That's Chris Potter, he's a junior at Dreher," the bartender said as he polished a wine glass. "He's underage, but we let him slip in on jazz nights."

"Is he any good?" I asked.

"Just wait," the bartender said as he moved off to help another customer.

About that time, Rosen ended his solo, the rest of the band kicked in and played the melody, and then the kid with the tenor sax tore into a solo of such amazing skill, I couldn't believe my ears. The timbre of his tone, the range of his imagination, and the dexterity in his touch were astonishing. This was the sound of a seasoned jazz player, I thought, not some kid from Dreher High School.

The bartender looked over at me from the other side of the bar, a huge smile on his face. He didn't have to say a thing.

That was my first encounter with Chris Potter but it certainly wouldn't be my last. I began going to Pug's to hear him play every chance I got, and while there I listened to what the other, older jazz musicians had to say about their young cohort.

"His energy level and emotional involvement are always there," said Rosen one night during a break between sets. "His musicianship and creativity are always there. He never disappoints you."

"He certainly has the talent and the right attitude, and he's able to assess situations well and use good judgment," added USC jazz professor Roger Pemberton. "He should be able to go as far as he wants."

I sat and listened to the accolades pour forth from Columbia's jazz cognoscenti almost 25 years ago, and I agreed with everyone. But at the time I doubt anyone who heard Potter play in Pug's could have imagined just exactly how far he would go in the world of jazz.

To date, Potter has recorded more than 15 albums as a bandleader. One, 1998's "Vertigo," was named one of the year's Top 10 jazz CDs by The New York Times. He has played on more than 150 CDs by other jazz artists. He was a guest artist on Steely Dan's Grammy-winning CD "Two Against Nature," and he toured the world with the legendary pop outfit, bringing audiences to their feet during his solo on "Aja."

Potter earned a Grammy nomination in 1999 for his performance on Joanne Brackeen's CD, "Pink Elephant Magic," and his own 2004 CD "Lift: Live at the Village Vanguard," was picked as one of the year's best jazz records by Fred Kaplan at Slate.

The list of awards, notable performances, and significant collaborations goes on and on. Potter is now 41, a seasoned performer far removed from that tousled-haired kid with the goofy grin back in Pug's all those years ago. But one thing has not changed, and that's his burning desire to explore every facet of the music and keep getting better and better. It's been that way ever since the summer before he entered fifth grade. That's when he heard Paul Desmond playing saxophone on Dave Brubeck's "Take Five" album and knew right away that he wanted to be a sax player.

Potter was born in Chicago, but while he was still an infant, his family moved to Columbia. His home was a place of love and support, where a variety of music -- everything from The Beatles to Debussy -- was played around the house.

"Even when he was a toddler, he loved music," says Chris's dad, David Potter. "He had a little Fisher-Price record player and played Mr. Rogers and Sesame Street records over and over. Then he started rummaging through our record collection."

Potter's talent emerged at an early age when a cheap little electric organ from the Kress store on Main Street was brought home, and the fourth grader took to it immediately. Then came the sound of Paul Desmond's saxophone, and that was that. He had to have a saxophone.

Since there were no music programs in the schools at that time, Potter's dad enlisted the help of a USC grad student named Bryson Borgstedt to teach his son the saxophone. From the first moment Borgstedt heard Potter play, he knew he was in the presence of an extraordinary talent, one that hovered on the realm of genius.

USC music professor Doug Graham remembers when Borgstedt knocked on his office door one day and told him he needed to come across the hall and hear this kid play. Potter played an original composition for Graham, who just stood there, astounded at what he was hearing.

"How old is he?" he asked Borgstedt.

"He's in the sixth grade," Borgstedt replied.

Word began to spread about Potter's enormous talent, as did the stories of his insight and intellect.

There was the time a USC professor invited Potter

to be a guest at his class of master and doctorate candidates in music. They were amazed by his playing and started asking him questions about how he learned music theory. Potter, who was a teenager by this time, went to the blackboard and said here are the chords to the song, but I like to use these chord substitutions.

"He started writing on the blackboard and left them all in the dust," Graham says. "Chris told me once that his dad bought him a book on music theory, but he never found time to read it."

Then there was the time the Dreher High concert band needed a bassoon player, so Potter checked out a bassoon, took it home and learned the fingering, and played the part the next day.

Once he went toe-to-toe with legendary clarinetist Eddie Daniels, and played Daniels' solo back to him note for note. The stories go on and on, but the most important and influential took place in 1986 when Potter was 15. For several years at the time, there was an annual jazz concert on Main Street in Columbia that featured an impressive array of jazz veterans from New York who would come down for the event. On the night before each concert, there was a traditional party where all the old friends would get together and jam and visit and have a good time. The 1986 party was attended by an array of jazz stars, including pianist Marian McPartland, guitarist Bucky Pizzarelli, and trumpeter Red Rodney. Potter was there, too, and when he was invited to sit in with the veterans, everyone kind of smiled and said, OK, we'll let the local kid have a shot.

I said, 'What is this kid going to do?'" McPartland remembers. "But he was wonderful. I was absolutely thrilled. I said, 'Gosh, this kid should be playing with Woody Herman,' but his father was standing there and said, 'Not until he finishes school!'"

Rodney was so impressed, he told the young saxophonist that if he was ever in New York, he should give him a call. The gleam in Potter's eye suggested he planned to do just that.

One year after the night I first heard him play in Pug's, Potter was named the nation's best high school jazz instrumental soloist by *Down Beat* magazine, the music's most authoritative voice. Potter had entered a cassette tape in the competition and was chosen from more than 900 entries. He was also chosen as a Presidential Scholar in the Arts, and he played at the Kennedy Center that summer of 1989. He was the only jazz artist invited.

Potter was no longer just the hot hometown jazz player. His talent had been widely recognized, and there was only one place for him to go: New York City. So in the fall of 1989, he moved north to enroll in the New School for Social Research. He studied at the New School for a year before transferring to the Manhattan School of Music, where he graduated in 1993.

But he had made that call to Red Rodney as soon as he unpacked his suitcases on arriving in New York, and the old trumpeter immediately enlisted him to be in his band. So between classes during those four years, Potter was playing gigs around town, rubbing shoulders with every jazz player he could meet, and even touring the world with Rodney when schedules permitted.

During one such tour, the owner of a record label in Holland was so knocked out by Potter's playing, he offered the 21-year-old a record deal. This led to Potter's first album as a bandleader, a CD titled "Presenting Chris Potter" on the Criss Cross label.

But Potter had little time to enjoy his debut release. In August of 1993, Potter's phone rang, and it was a representative from the band Steely Dan, who was planning the group's first tour in more than two decades. Would it be possible, the caller asked, if Potter might join the band and play tenor sax?

So off he went on a sold-out world tour with Steely Dan.

"We did three nights in Madison Square Garden," Potter says. "Sold out everywhere. It was wild to walk onstage and hear the sound of 20,000 people cheering."

The tour was such a huge success, Steely Dan decided to do it again in 1995, and once again they asked Potter to play in the horn section. But surprisingly, he turned them down. He decided to play small jazz clubs in Europe that summer with the drummer Paul Motian.

"Those are the kind of risks you take that end up paying off in a weird way," he said a few years later. "That was a hundred percent the right decision to make, because I was able to grow as a musician."

And that has been the driving force behind Potter's musical journey from the very beginning: to learn everything he can about the music, and continue to get better and better.

Over the years, Potter has talked about developing his own musical language and "honing in on what I want to say." He understands the deep complexity of jazz and the depth of its history, from Louis Armstrong to Lester Young to Charlie Parker to John Coltrane.

"And it keeps adding on," he says. "You have to know the beginning, the foundation, then move forward and go beyond it."

These days, Potter has moved way beyond the dreams of that kid who used to sneak into Pug's on Tuesday nights. He has recorded and performed with some of the leading names in jazz, including Herbie Hancock, Dave Holland, John Scofield, Jim Hall, and many others. Down Beat recently called him "one of the most studied (and copied) saxophonists on the planet," and the magazine's readers voted Potter second only to tenor sax legend Sonny Rollins in the 2008 *Down Beat* readers' poll.

Chris Potter is indeed a saxophone colossus, and it's not unreasonable to include his name on a list of influential jazz stars that would include Young, Parker, Rollins, Wayne Shorter, and Paul Desmond, the saxophonist who inspired the young Rosewood Elementary student all those years ago.

Columbia guitarist Jim Mings once remarked that Potter "moved from Shandon to Times

Square and fit in perfectly in both places." And it's true. Potter still has the goofy grin and a laidback, likable persona, but now he is an artist of international renown. He will keep honing his sound and searching for new avenues of artistic expression. He will remain open to discovery, and he'll keep striving to be a better musician. (Currently, Potter is touring as part of Pat Metheny's band, and the guitarist is thrilled to have him, having said that Potter is "one of the greatest musicians I have ever been around.")

Once during a deep conversation in a café in Atlanta, Potter and I were talking about the pros and cons of different musical genres and how each had its own unique rewards. He talked about keeping your mind, eyes, and ears open to the subtle emotions in every art form.

Then he turned to me and said, "What is an artist doing? Trying to describe to you what it feels like to be alive."

Could there be a higher calling? Maybe, but I don't think so.

I am certain, however, that when you hear Chris Potter play the saxophone, you feel truly alive.

Blue Sky

Public Artist

"We are an odd people. We make it as difficult as possible for our artists to work honestly while they are alive; either we refuse them money or we ruin them with money; either we flatter them with unhelpful praise or wound them with unhelpful blame, and when they are too old, or too dead, or too beyond dispute to hinder any more, we canonize them so that what was wild is tamed, what was objecting, becomes Authority."

Jeanette Winterson, Art Objects, 1995

By Cynthia Boiter

It's a particularly hot summer day, even for Columbia, when I parallel park my car on Washington Street and notice a tall, lanky gentleman as he moves stiffly to reposition an oversized canvas by the curb. Dressed smartly in pressed pants, long sleeved shirt, jacket, and his ever-present dapper chapeau, the aging artist wears more clothes than most anyone on the street—even the bankers have rolled up their sleeves—as he daubs a cloth soaked in aromatic chemicals across the face of what appears to be a perfectly good painting to distress it. Even when wrestling with the kind of unruly canvas that would cause someone a third of his age to curse and spit, Columbia's ever-present artist-in-residence stubbornly maintains his sense of style and composure. He may have grown up and, let's face it, grown old in Columbia; he may have cycled into and out of fashion as the decades have worn on, only to shift back into the limelight once again; he may have met as many foes as fans along his journey; but as an elder in the Columbia community of artists and urban dwellers, the visual artist Blue Sky has consistently and uniquely personified the meaning of cool, all-the-while remaining devoted to the city he adores.

A child of the Depression, Sky was born Warren Edward Johnson on September 18, 1938, and attended Dreher High School, then the University of South Carolina where he earned his bachelor's and master's degrees in art and education. His childhood was spent in poverty but his artistic proclivities presented themselves early and, as a boy, he drew everything from abstract sketches to World War II aircraft in precise detail.

The impact of having early mentors in his corner isn't lost on the artist and, even today, he fondly recalls his high school art teacher, Moselle Skinner, who introduced him to the Abstract Expressionism she had learned about during her studies in New York City. Recognizing his almost precocious talent, Skinner offered Sky his own art studio behind the school's art room and made it available to him at any time. It was while in this private studio that Sky first began to paint with oils and, ultimately, to leave the studio behind to experiment with techniques in *plein air* painting – a practice in which he continues to delight.

"Nothing rivals the experience of painting outside on location," Sky says. "I do it now and I think about the Impressionists and the direction that those innovators took art in back then; it amazes me. Impressionism may well have been the greatest period in painting because of the way it opened people up to seeing the beauty in everything around them."

Sky reminisces about his early days of *plein air* painting when he was one of a gang of young Columbia artists who would pile into cars carrying paints, easels, wine, beer, and bread.

"We would head out to the park and paint for hours, and some of those paintings actually turned out pretty good," he says. "Besides, there's nothing more fun than partying with a group of artists." To this day it's unusual to find Sky without either a paint brush or a glass of wine in his hand.

Much of Sky's success at the university can also be credited to his mentor and chairperson of the Art Department, Edmund Yaghjian. "He was a well-known and immensely talented artist and we would sit for hours in Yaghjian's office just talking and looking at art magazines," Sky remembers. "One afternoon I was sitting in his office reading a magazine and Yaghjian walked in and wanted to know why I wasn't in class." As stubborn then as he is now, the young artist was hesitant to admit the truth to his mentor, but he finally broke down and confessed that he "didn't have the money for tuition. Yaghjian reached for his checkbook and handed me a check, and that's how I went to school that semester."

It was also Yaghjian who got Sky his first New York job in 1961 illustrating books for Harper New York; an exacting practice that taught the young artist that he was less interested in precision design and more interested in being true to his own artistic purpose. "I think Yaghjian planned it that way," Sky says, cutting his gaze to the corner of his eye and smiling.

Though courted by the likes of Henry Geldzahler, curator of the Metropolitan Museum of Art, who had encountered Sky's work when he judged the Sixth Annual Spring Mills Art Contest in 1964, awarding Sky the prize for Best in Show, the artist stayed true to Columbia where he felt most at home.

"I went to New York during the summer of 1964, and Geldzahler took me around, and I met the people he wanted me to meet. But they didn't really impress me," he skeptically recalls. "I knew I was meeting people who were important and who, I guess could have helped me out in my career. But I didn't like the lifestyle—we weren't communicating. I just never felt comfortable."

Sky returned to New York City the next year, however, and worked there as an industrial design draftsman for wages on which he could barely subsist while studying at the illustrious Art Students League of New York. The crowds and noise of the city bothered him though and his long mass transit commute took time away from his art. In April, a long and disappointing Sunday afternoon drive to the city's nearby Jones Beach, with its traffic and small, overcrowded plots of sand, proved to be the last straw for the young Southerner who, the next day, resigned from his job, packed his belongings in his car, and headed straight home to the shores of South Carolina.

"It was like a rebirth for me," he remembers. "At 27, I'd always dreamed that one day I would be a New York artist painting in an apartment somewhere, happy, and productive. I expected it, and maybe I was on the way to making it happen, but it didn't feel right. I don't think it ever would have." Sky drove directly to Pawley's Island where he just stood on the sand that stretched as far as he could see and then, driving home to Columbia, cried almost all of the way.

But the experience of living and working in New York served him well. "It told me something—how much I love South Carolina," Sky says. "A lot of people blame their failures on where they live. They think that if only they lived in a more progressive place or if only the people around them were different, that their lives would be different, too. Suddenly they would be successful and happy and everything would be perfect. I'm here to say, 'not necessarily.'"

Sky could have moved away at any time, put down roots anywhere, but he didn't. He stayed.

Back home, Sky attended graduate school at what was then USC's Hilton Head Island arts campus, working in watercolors and devoting himself to representational art—his subject almost always being the Southern landscape he had so bitterly missed while in New York. In 1967, he staged his first solo show at Columbia's now defunct Laurel Gallery, and in 1970 he painted his first truck back of notice—literally a painting of the rear of an industrial vehicle and the first of many automotive creations to come. The painting was chosen for inclusion in the 1970 American Watercolor Society exhibition in New York City, despite the artist's absence from the organization's official ranks. Similarly, *Cream Puff*, a painting of a 1957 Cadillac, was presented the Purchase Award in 1971's Springs Mills Show and deemed by the adjudicator, Perry Rathbone, director of the Boston Museum of Fine Arts, to be "a distinguished work ... subtle and poetic."

By the early seventies, Sky had become comfortable in the role of Columbia's resident artist, always dressed in dapper attire—white suits and Panama hats, for example—the kind of clothes few local men dared wear. But with his cool quotient firmly in place, the man entering his mid-thirties had the confidence to pull off a public persona that many considered eccentric, but most either admired or, at the very least, considered *interesting*.

It was an age of introspection and experimentation and the early part of the seventies was spent, for Sky, in a self-prescribed search for greater meaning in his life both in and outside of art. Over the years, he experimented with meditation, vegetarianism, celibacy, and drugs. Ultimately, Sky found himself, in many ways, an entirely new person. Having answered to the name Warren Johnson for over 35 years, in 1974 he legally changed his name to Blue Sky. "I felt like I was no longer the same person and I wanted my name to reflect that transformation," he says.

But changing his name wasn't enough. "I wanted to paint something that would embody a passageway for the transformation toward illumination that I had made in my own life, and I wanted to graphically demonstrate how most people see enlightenment," Sky explains. From this need to share the transformative process he had experienced, perhaps his most important painting was born: *Tunnelvision*—a 75 by 50 foot *trompe l'oeil* mural, and the first of its kind in South Carolina. "It literally came to me in a dream," Sky says.

The 1975 unveiling of the painting garnered international attention. The following year the mural was featured in *People Magazine* and *Readers Digest* and the artist was flooded with requests to give talks and create more murals. Uninterested in the attention, Sky left Columbia and took temporary refuge in a *Kriya* monastery in California. The Carmel area of California has since served often as an interim sanctuary for the artist who disdains publicity but loves his art and coming back to his home in Columbia.

Appropriately controversial, some of Sky's other local public art displays have either appeared seemingly out of nowhere, disappeared into the earth, or required his home town's not-always-patient art patrons to wait in exasperation for the unveiling.

Funded entirely by the artist himself, *NEVERBUST* is a 25 foot long chain of welded steel links that are 5 feet in diameter and stretch between two historic buildings on Columbia's Main Street. Though Sky had the consent of the building owners to create the installation, he had the savvy to realize that the city might delay or even censor him if he went through the proper channels for approval of such a project. Early on a Sunday morning in 2000, he crept onto Main Street and installed the pre-constructed sculpture as a surprise to the city. When the project finally went before the Landmark's Commission it was unanimously approved.

Busted Plug Plaza, on the other hand, which was installed in 2001, was a project kept under the wraps of a giant gray tarp for the 14 months it took to complete the sculpture. Weighing in at 675,000 pounds and more than four stories high, the sculpture of the fire hydrant in the center of the plaza, located in the *Tunnelvision* parking lot along Taylor Street, qualifies as the world's largest.

Kawasakisaurus was a 2003 site-specific sculpture installation in Columbia's Vista on the corner of Senate and Pulaski Streets, on land owned by South Carolina Bank and Trust. Constructed from 16 carefully positioned abandoned motorcycles and a Volkswagen Beetle fender, all encrusted with cement and then painted the color of bleached bones, *Kawasakisaurus* created the illusion of an archeological dig site for a fossilized dinosaur. In 2007, representatives from the bank consulted Sky about moving the art—created specifically for that location—to a new home along the South Carolina coast. After a period of failed negotiations, the artist instructed bank officials to simply cover his work up with sod rather than move it, which, appallingly, they did.

Today, it's hard to find a local arts aficionado who doesn't have an opinion on the work of Blue Sky, particularly the public art pieces addressed in this essay. Most either love them, or they hate them. And even those who are indifferent at least recognize the fact that the art—specific pieces of art—are there in places where no art was before.

And here we have it. Three things, among others, that one of Columbia's earliest contemporary artists did for the city in which he grew up, the city in which he grew old: He stayed; he gave us the most important thing he had to give—his art; and he set a precedent. In other words, he did for his generation, long before the term "creative class" had slipped from the lips of Richard

Florida, exactly what we ask of this generation of Columbians today. Stay. Give us your talent. Set an example for others to follow.

At print time for this compendium, the artist Blue Sky, once again, finds himself in the position of being forced to argue for the continued existence of one of his creations. *Busted Plug Plaza,* discussed earlier, is in danger of being displaced, or worse, as land owners more interested in money than the preservation of the modest arts landscape of our city, would have him abandon his art or have it moved to another location. This begs two questions. Once *Busted Plug Plaza* is gone, what is there to protect the vista of the mural *Tunnelvision,* which sits practically in the great fire hydrant's shadow; will it be the next piece of public art targeted? And, just as important, what message does the disposal or displacement of a local icon's creation send to the young artists who we hope will follow the example he so generously set?

It's all about value.

Hanging in the halls of the Smithsonian Institution, The White House, and the homes of unlikely collectors like Henry Kissinger and others who value his work—hanging in many of *our* homes—are original paintings by Columbia artist, Blue Sky. To read about his work in English, consult the pages of such respected periodicals as *The Christian Science Monitor, Oxford American, House and Garden, National Geographic,* and dozens more ranging from *Penthouse* to *Weekly*

Reader. But to read about his work in other languages, you would have to be fluent in Greek, Italian, Dutch, German, Swedish, Flemish, and Chinese—the languages where Sky's work is valued throughout the world.

It shouldn't have to be said that there is value in an artist's work, whether we like that work or not, and there is value in the artist who created it. But clearly, for some of us, it does. The value of Sky's contribution to our local culture goes beyond the inherent quality of his work to include the precedents he set and the choices he made. In addition to his murals and paintings in collections far and wide, the legacy of Blue Sky, specific to Columbians, are pieces of public art that make us think, agree, disagree, and sometimes change our minds. Rather than even considering casting a piece aside, shouldn't we be asking the artist for more?

Pat Conroy

How I Stalked My Prince of Tides

By Janna McMahan

It began with a gift.

In 1987, my new husband and I moved from Kentucky to South Carolina. Before we left, my mother-in-law gave me a popular book set along the coast of my new state. Having gone to college in South Carolina, she appreciated this novel's descriptions of the land and culture.

Years later, while I was going through cancer treatment, I found *The Prince of Tides* in a long-forgotten box. I have always been a reader, sometimes devouring a book in one day, but this time it took me a while to get started. I kept rereading the prologue, admiring the beautiful construction of the sentences. I was struck by how the author injected wonder into the story one moment and filled the page with dread the next. He had me studying the elegance of his execution rather than just rolling along with the plot.

I was prone to introspection that winter of my illness. I was only 28. If I had limited time, what would I want to accomplish?

I made a list. In no particular order I wrote:

1) Trip around the world.

2) Own a convertible.

3) Write a novel.

When my treatment was over, my husband and I joined friends on a trek through Thailand and India. We flew always west eventually encircling the globe. When I returned I bought a white Miata, a lovely little ride I still enjoy.

My health continued to improve. Precious days ticked by moving me toward that five-year mark where cancer patients begin to believe in the future again.

One day I received an unexpected delivery. Inside the box was a laptop with a note from my brother.

No excuses. Write that book.

I gathered the nerve to quit my public relations job at an art museum and set out to become a writer. I had written about visual art for years, so it was a natural transition to freelance writing. I had no problem getting assignments from editors who remembered my media releases.

As my portfolio of magazine clips grew, so did my attempts at writing fiction. I wrote a number of short stories and a novel that I felt had good bones but lacked something in execution. I took a fiction class and formed a writing group with other students who brought snippets of work they admired. Often the name Pat Conroy came up. He had become a notorious figure by then, his work widely admired, his politics derided, his personal life a sad sore.

One night after group, I was drawn to my bookshelf where I tilted the familiar salt marsh cover of *The Prince of Tides* toward me and the Lowcountry slipped into my hands. Here again was that amazing prologue, a singularly beautiful piece of literature. If I could be a writer, I wanted to be descriptive like Pat Conroy. I wanted such a felicity of language and the ability to paint fertile landscapes with words.

One day my group took a trip to a nearby burg to hear Pat Conroy speak. Unlike so many authors, he didn't read from his novels. He told stories. You could tell entertaining was in his DNA. He had an "aw shucks" way about him; *I'm one of you* his approach implied. Afterward, I waited in line for an hour before shyly offering my tattered book for his signature.

His performance that night made me realize that being an author wasn't just about writing. It was also about being a personality able to captivate an audience. I'd seen a number of authors speak, but until I saw Pat Conroy I'd never seen it done right.

My goal became to interview him. I contacted his publicist who sent me a galley copy of *My Losing Season,* his new book that was many months away from release. I pitched the story idea to my editor at *Charleston* magazine and she bought it.

I hadn't anticipated was how difficult it would be to get in touch with the author. He didn't have a website and working through his publicist didn't pan out. I started contacting people I thought would know him. Folks at the South Carolina Arts Commission claimed a connection, but refused me his number or address. Bookstore owners also felt the need to protect that information. That was when I saw the poster, a glorious stroke of fortune. Pat Conroy was to speak at the student center at the University of South Carolina.

After his talk at USC, I boldly approached him before he could get behind the signing desk where he would be for an hour or more.

"Mr. Conroy," I blurted out. "I read *My Losing Season*. I'd love to interview you for *Charleston* magazine."

He turned to me. "Really? How did you get my new book?"

"Your publicist."

He smiled and his blue, blue eyes focused on me. Then he said, "Why of course young lady. I would be most pleased to have you interview me."

"I don't know how to get in touch with you, sir. Everybody feels as if they need to protect you."

He laughed at that and motioned for me to hand him my note pad. He scribbled down his number.

"Give me a call and we'll talk." Then his people whisked him away.

I spent the next few weeks reading his novels. I amassed a sizable file of articles on him and began to notice a pattern to his interviews. He spoke foremost of his family, his abusive father and frustrating mother, and how a traumatic childhood was a great asset to a writer. As a PR person, I appreciated his understanding of platform and how to stay on point, but I didn't want the same interview he had given to others. I read and formulated questions I felt had gone unasked.

The next day I left my request for an interview on his answering machine. Weeks passed. I left more messages.

One day my phone rang and I was surprised to hear that precise, clipped voice.

"This is Pat Conroy. Would this be the tenacious Ms. McMahan who is looking to interview me?"

I always tried to speak with visual artists in their studios. To see a person's workspace allows for a better sense of them as an artist, so I asked if I could to talk him in person. He agreed and we set a date.

As I pulled up to his sea island home I was prepared, but nervous. Never before had I interviewed someone whose work I admired so much. I wanted to learn about how to be an author from this literary superstar.

The door was answered by his wife, novelist Cassandra King. Her wide, gentle smile seemed to say that I was welcome and I immediately felt better.

She showed me to the living room where I shook hands with my subject and we settled into a comfortable sofa. I pulled out my new sleek digital recorder and my note pad.

As I set up he said, "So how did you get this interview with me?"

I paused. He didn't remember meeting me and our telephone conversation?

"I met you after your lecture at USC. You gave me your phone number." He nodded slightly and I was glad to move on. "Is it okay if I tape this?"

"That will be fine. I've never seen one of those. What is that?"

"Digital recorder. You don't have to switch out tapes."

I fumbled with the controls. After a number of failed attempts I silently cursed myself for not having practiced with it more than I had.

"Not to worry. I have my cassette recorder in the car," I said.

"And here I was prepared to be so impressed by you," he said. This startled me, but then I saw his eyes snap and a grin pull at the corners of his mouth.

Aware that his time was valuable I delved right in with questions. He was eloquent and forthcoming, but I noticed when he began to nudge the conversation in a direction I recognized.

I decided to take a chance. "I recognize that story from other articles I've read about you. Can you tell me something you haven't told anyone else? Something new and fresh?"

He studied me and I thought I'd crossed the line. Then he said, "Let's get out of here. I'll give you my Beaufort tour."

The floorboard of his luxury sedan was littered with fast food cups, newspapers and magazines.

"Just throw all that in the back," he said.

As we headed toward the mainland I clicked on my trusty old recorder and began again with questions.

At one point he said, "You're very prepared. Most people who interview me have read only one of my books at best."

He talked about people showing up on his doorstep unannounced. Even though he lives in a gated community, numerous strangers have rung his doorbell. I suddenly understood his earlier question about how I had gotten the interview. In his world, it paid to be cautious.

He talked about how he had no patience for writers who whined about the difficulty of writing. He insisted it was all good, from the solitude of writing to the speaking gigs to the hours of book signings. We talked about his recent foray in magazine writing for *Gourmet* and *Southern Living*. When I expressed surprise that he would do magazine work he simply said, "I see no downside to going to the finest restaurants, eating the best food and writing about it."

He gave me the history, architecture, and Hollywood tour of Beaufort. As his car crawled the heavily shaded streets of his chocolate box town, he pointed out local landmarks like the sturdy fireproof house and the house with the eye-lid window. We stopped at one Georgian-style house he called The Cat lady House where hundreds of cats, both dead and alive, were found inside after the owner's demise.

"Some were in the freezer," he said. "You couldn't write that stuff."

He pointed out where the movies for *The Great Santini* and *The Prince of Tides* were shot. He showed me where his mother gave him a book party for his first novel. He took me to the cemetery where his parents lay. He spoke to the neighboring interred as if they were family. When we reached The Great Santini's grave he said, "Hello, Dad."

We spent the afternoon talking about the writing life and what makes good literature. He said to be prepared for readers to share their own painful stories. He also warned me to be cautious of self-censorship.

"We are our own worst censors. We won't write anything that we think will hurt people, so we water things down. Don't do that. Be brave. Write about things nobody is willing to talk about. That's where story lives."

I have interviewed Pat twice since. I suppose it is fair to say we are professional friends. Both he and Cassandra are always gracious to ask me about my own writing when I run into them at book events.

My day with Pat stoked my ambition. He made being an author seem like a logical dream. I wasn't crazy. I was a writer. That year I wrote my first novel. *Calling Home* rapidly found an agent, publisher and commercial success.

So, I didn't really stalk Pat Conroy. I just wanted to meet my literary idol and I went for it. I wanted to be a writer and he told me how do it.

If you are in need of inspiration for your artistic endeavors, I highly recommend spending the day with Pat Conroy. But don't ask me for his contact information. I'm sorry, but I just can't give that out.

James Busby

Layers of Talent

By Jeffrey Day

When I first came across James Busby's art—paintings made of layers of white gesso which has been grooved and polished to the sheen of marble—it was a true sense of discovery that doesn't often come along. Rarely does one stumble upon such an accomplished young artist making great art in the space above his suburban garage. My only regret was that I didn't know about him earlier. By the time our paths crossed in 2005 he was already showing in New York.

The artist, who grew up in Rock Hill, has since moved on from white, although gesso is still an important part of his art making. After the white pieces, he created a black series made in a similar manner, but with the final layer painstakingly applied with small sticks of graphite. These ranged from flat deep gray that seemed to absorb all light to others with a mirror-like surface. They looked more like lead or steel than marble. Early 2012 found him working in other new ways. Instead of cutting the surfaces of dried gesso, he was making marks in the wet paint with trowels and other tools. To this point most of the artist's paintings were moderately sized – from one to two feet in width and height – but now he went big creating a batch of multi-paneled works the largest of which measured 8-by-

12 feet. These pieces were much more painterly with elaborate surfaces of arcs and swirls and indentations, but still retaining marks of mechanical precision. Nor were they white or black, but more of a gray.

Brian Lang, former decorative arts curator at the Columbia Museum of Art and now chief curator of the Arkansas Art Center, first saw Busby's art in the home of a local collection when putting together the *Carolina Collects* exhibition in 2008. Like me, he was bowled over.

"I was immediately taken with it," says Lang. "I wondered 'Why he isn't better known?' I can't think of many others doing what he is doing."

Not long ago I received an email from Busby saying that someone had broken into his studio and vandalized his art. Fortunately he was kidding. It's just that the new painting had a lot of color and bright color. (Color showed up – or more accurately showed through – in some of his earlier pieces, but not often.)

Still whether white, black, gray, or these non-colors with green, purple and orange, his aesthetic and technical approach is unmistakable.

When I first visited Busby he was living in a new subdivision off St. Andrews Road with his wife Karen and their daughter. (Another daughter was on the way and a son would follow a couple of years later.) It could have been anyone's well-appointed home with nice furniture and a recently redecorated kitchen, but with better art.

The second floor of the garage though was a

sanctuary of art making. The entire room was white with the floor coated with a thick layer of dried gesso, the basic white paint applied to provide a neutral and smooth surface for a painter to work on. In-progress pieces were perched on buckets and boxes, the edges of the wooden panels dripping stalagmites of dried gesso. After putting down the many coats of gesso, Busby would carry the panels down the narrow stairway to the first floor of the garage and place them face down on a table saw, rather blindly cutting grooves into the thick surface. He'd then carefully sand and burnish the works, making a final pass with tissue paper producing a glowing, alabaster-like surface. The pieces were officially painting, but with the cut channels, curving surfaces, and sometimes larger openings they were just as much sculpture.

To me the paintings were simply beautiful. Although monochromatic, they were hardly simple, crisscrossed as they were with grooves and fragile cliffs of paint. Even the small ones had a commanding presence. I always admire artists—be they painters or writers or composers—who can do a great deal with very little and that's what I saw with Busby's work. The craftsmanship, for which I am a sucker, was impeccable. Not surprisingly, Busby also admires artists who concentrate on a narrow body of work such as Emilio Morandi who painted the same grouping of bottles and vases for decades on end.

"I love artists who can sustain a body of work like that over time," he says. "How does one do something simple really well?"

One can respect and like Busby's art in the multitude of ways it is possible to respect and like art. The work stands on its own, but the process is also an important part of the appreciation of the work, even when it is mostly a mystery to the viewer. The artworks look as if he came up with a detailed plan for each, but Busby creates them in a very intuitive manner. In addition, it can be difficult to determine not only how they are made, but what they are made of. All this gives depth and breadth and an unexpected emotional charge to the austere pieces.

"I like work that makes you think about something completely different than what's hanging on the wall," Busby says. "I like art that makes you reconsider what you always thought you knew. I love work I can't figure out right away."

Busby came to the white works—and all that would follow since—during a difficult time. He had started on his master's degree in fine arts at Virginia Commonwealth University in Richmond where he was making huge red paintings with floating images of disembodied limbs tied directly to his mother's battle with cancer. After she died in 2002, he began doing paintings of cows that looked over the fence near the family home in York County. They were still, he felt, about his mother. Over time, the cows grew smaller, began disappearing. He had come to the end of that road, but had no idea where to go next, not a good place for someone entering their last year of graduate school. Or maybe, as it turned out, a very good place.

Not knowing what to do, Busby began doing

something that he disliked: stretching canvases and putting layers of gesso on them.

"I always hated that—I wanted to get to the main event, which was painting," he says.

Instead, he found this fairly mindless preliminary work meditative.

"The actual coating process is like this ritualistic thing," Busby says. "It's almost this strange little dance working around the pieces. And it is a very controlled act."

With a studio full of stretched and primed canvases, he contemplated what to do with them.

"Just out of curiosity I started sanding them and when I did that they'd develop this nice surface that didn't look like canvas," Busby says. "I'd been wanting to cut them for a year, but I couldn't get up the nerve. When I cut the first one I knew this was what I needed to do."

He picked a good time to start cutting. Each year Virginia Commonwealth organizes a New York exhibition for its students curated by someone from the city's art community. In 2002 that was Stefan Stux, owner of Stux Gallery in the Chelsea arts district. He was impressed with Busby's pieces and the following year included him in a show. The gallery has mounted solo shows by the artist nearly every year since 2005.

"He impressed me as someone energetic, passionate and smart," Stux says. "It took me some time to realize how creative and smart he really is."

Works in the exhibitions generally sold well and he also came to the attention of Hubert Neumann who is usually on the list of the world's Top 100 art collectors every year. Neumann has purchased a number of Busby's pieces and included him in group shows in New York and Paris.

Over the summer of 2012, Busby made a difficult career decision, leaving Stux Gallery for Kravets/Wehby gallery a few blocks away. He was added to the list of gallery artists on August 7 and his first solo exhibition opened five weeks later.

"I love the pressure it presents," he says. "It allows you to not overthink the work."

The pressure appears to have worked; seven of the eleven paintings sold the first weekend.

―――

About a year ago, the Busby family moved into a bigger house in another, even newer subdivision on the edges of Chapin. The artist also set up a new and huge studio in what was once the shop and office of a boat builder. It doesn't have the magical quality of that tiny above-the-garage room, but it does give him more room to work and is large enough for him to hang the paintings and let him see what they might look like in a gallery space. There's also enough space for the kids to camp out, play, and make art with their dad.

Having young children has made its mark on the art indirectly and directly.

"I think I'm embracing the madness of having three little kids," he says.

Over the summer, Busby volunteered to do some paintings for their vacation Bible school. There was a lot of leftover paint and it was quite colorful. He filled containers of orange, red, green, and purple and took them to the studio. Not only did they provide color, but an element of chance.

"I didn't even choose the colors," he says. "It's a big jump when I've seen nothing but shades of gray and white for 10 years. I want to be surprised when I come in here. It's very liberating. Post-show is a time when I'm in the experimental stage. It's exciting to shuffle the deck and see what comes up. I need to see how I can squirm my way out of this. I think all good artists do this. You look at the work and see how it's challenging you."

―

I've been writing about the arts for nearly three decades and have been lucky, and I hope perceptive enough, to realize when I've come across mostly unknown, but amazing artists. It doesn't happen often nor should it, because there aren't that many amazing artists. James Busby is undoubtedly one of them.

Marjory Wentworth

Laureate

By Kristine Hartvigsen

As she sat stunned in her car on Charleston's rickety old John P. Grace Memorial Bridge, trapped precariously 150 feet above the swift-moving waters of the Cooper River, Marjory Wentworth said there was no proverbial flash reel of her life playing through her mind, just terror and paralyzing shock at the sheer violence of the crash on an otherwise perfect fall day in 2004.

"We were not allowed to get out of the car because it was right on the edge," she tells me. "Another inch or two, and our car would have been over the side. It was a very scary thing."

I could imagine the traffic inching along the bridge, gawking at the accident. Who knew it was South Carolina's Poet Laureate in that car resting so vulnerably on the edge of the aging bridge. Fortunately, Wentworth and her husband, Peter—while shaken—were physically alright. Already, construction had begun on the modern new Arthur Ravenel, Jr. Bridge to replace the deteriorating Depression-era bridge (as well as its neighboring span, the Silas Pearman Bridge). And the following year, the City of Charleston invited Wentworth to compose a poem celebrating the opening of the iconic new Ravenel Bridge. Over several years, she had watched the erection of its massive, diamond-shaped towers, with a sense of awe.

"What interested me were the workers," she says. Many were migrants, and one of them—Miguel Angel Rojas Lucas of Mexico—fell to his death during construction of one of the towers. "The young man who died was the same age as one of my sons." Inspiration for the bridge poem emerged from her advocacy for refugees and worldwide human rights. The resulting poem, *Despite Gravity*, honors those from distant lands who come to America in pursuit of dreams, the bridge's iconic towers serving as beacons for hope.

They come, because a bridge is like a dream
of what is possible. It rises from the earth
as if gravity was something imagined,
and the forces of the universe were suspended.
Workers take plywood and steel, construct a framework
into the endless air, where cables holding
a million pounds of iron and concrete
are as elegant as strings on a harp
playing the sounds of wind rising off water.
  —from *Despite Gravity*

While in college, Wentworth completed an overseas fellowship at the United Nations High Commission for Refugees in Geneva, where she became immersed in refugee issues from Somalia to Cambodia. Upon returning home, while attending graduate school by night, the Massachusetts native worked by day helping displaced refugees from around the world resettle and adjust to life in the United States. She was inspired by their personal stories of survival and perseverance.

While studying for her master's degree in literature and creative writing at New York University, Wentworth enjoyed access to world-renowned writers, including poet Carolyn Forché, a human rights advocate who focused her most praised writings on the Salvadoran Civil War. Forché's award-winning work—particularly the world-famous prose poem "Colonel"—has been credited with making political issues deeply personal for people and coining the term "poetry of witness" to communicate the human costs of war and oppression.

Making these types of connections through powerful writing based on real people is critical to bringing attention to human rights abuses. At a conference, Wentworth heard Juan Méndez recall his 18-month detainment in Buenos Aires during Argentina's "Dirty War" in the 1970s. He had been imprisoned for defending human rights in the midst of genocide waged under Jorge Rafael Videla, who sought to eliminate any citizens who opposed his policies. As many as 20,000 citizens mysteriously "disappeared" during Videla's reign. While detained, Méndez was subjected to beatings and torture by electric prod before being expelled in 1977 and moving to the United States as a "Prisoner of Conscience" adopted by Amnesty International.

Moved by Méndez's remarks, Wentworth engaged him in conversation, and the two became longtime friends. Méndez went on to become the United Nations' Special Rapporteur on Torture and law professor at The American University's Washington College of Law. A book publicist, Wentworth later was named South Carolina Poet Laureate in 2003. The two stayed in touch over the years and eventually collaborated on a powerful non-fiction book titled *Taking a Stand: The Evolution of Human Rights*, which was published in 2011 by Palgrave Macmillan.

"It started out as the story of Juan's life, and, through the process of the writing the proposal, we developed the idea of interweaving his life and life's work into human rights themes," Wentworth says. She is particularly encouraged by the awareness of human rights issues she sees in young people almost everywhere, and she thinks the recent Occupy movement has emboldened many.

"As a human story, it is redemptive. Somebody who has suffered so much for what he believes in and come out to rebuild his life like Juan has is amazing," Wentworth says. "For me, to always be able to look at a human rights situation and evaluate what is happening provides a lot of clarity. I really don't understand how people make decisions without that. No matter what the situation is, torture has never solved anything. It really has more to do with sadism and Nazi scare tactics. When it happens, it takes a toll on the morality of a place. It's unnecessary and has to do with the worst in human behavior. ... I think a writer has to bear witness. For someone like me, it's part of why I write."

*Something hot passes over her head. It feels
like her hair is on fire, but she knows the sound
of mortars and the smell that follows.
Before she has time to run and grab her sons, a shell
explodes in the middle of the berry field. The sky
fills with smoke and a brief hard silence.*
    —from In Gaza's Berry Fields

Wentworth observes that Americans tend to believe that human rights abuses take place only in faraway places that are steeped in conflict and political instability. "I suggest we look around our own country and consider the human rights of people with no access to health care or a decent job," she writes in her blog. "Let's consider how we treat one another, especially the disenfranchised."

In her blog discussing Human Rights Day in 2011, Wentworth expresses despair at what she sees as an emerging culture of hostility in the United States. "There is a frightening acceptance of violence and cruelty in our society," she writes. "The new overzealous immigration laws proposed in South Carolina and other states are overtly racist and remind me of the policies of interning Japanese Americans during World War

II. ... No one's rights should be determined by their sexuality, gender, religion, political beliefs, or country of origin."

As an aspiring writer who reveres celebrated scribes and imagines their lives as near perfect, I was stunned to learn that Wentworth struggles with the same issues most of us do. She worries about paying the mortgage, about health insurance, about the fat content of foods, about college tuition for two sons and acceptance for a third with special needs, about an occasionally untidy house or untended garden. Being poet laureate is not as glamorous as less-accomplished writers might imagine. It is an unpaid position that's basically volunteer work. It neither contributes to the household bottom line nor adds hours to an already full day. It is a sacrifice, albeit a happy one.

As poet laureate, Wentworth represents the state at official events and composes poems for special observances, specifically the governor's inauguration. The position comes with constant requests to speak at commencements and special events. Wentworth continues her day job, teaching creative writing full-time at the Art Institute of Charleston and at Burke High School. She also serves on the boards of the Lowcountry Initiative for the Literary Arts (LILA), the Poetry Society of South Carolina, the University of South Carolina Poetry Initiative, and the Yo Art Project. In addition, she and her husband continue to run their publicity firm, Wentworth PR. It leaves little time to actually write new poetry or simply bask in her achievements. With diminishing opportunities in South Carolina for her film producer husband and the everyday cost-of-living grind we all face, Wentworth feels pressure to constantly work.

"I work 15 to 16 hours a day, every single day," she laments. "I would love to be able to work more just on writing. I love to teach, and I am really glad I got this job because we have health insurance now. But my goal would be to just have a life where I could spend more time writing."

Perhaps more than anything, Wentworth wants to use her poet laureate title to enrich and educate. Early in life, Wentworth found healing in poetry as she dealt with chronic childhood health issues that isolated her during long periods of bed rest and losing her father to cancer when she was just 14. He had instilled in Wentworth a love of literature and, especially, poetry. Writing became therapy, a tool for processing her grief and related emotions.

"I was lucky enough to have writing as an outlet when my dad was dying. Poetry is a vehicle for intense emotions," she says, adding that people need to feel safe in expressing themselves and working through complex feelings. So Wentworth founded the "Expressions of Healing" program at Roper Hospital and teaches cancer patients through journaling and poetry.

"It is a great privilege to teach those students. I learn a lot from them. There is a lot of wisdom and a lot of heart and a lot of humor," Wentworth says. "I still am amazed that I am paid to go in and work with them. It's like hearing a good sermon for two hours."

Wentworth recovered from her childhood ailments to become a high school athlete and later studied modern dance at Mt. Holyoke College. She even aspired for a while to choreograph and dance professionally. After moving to South Carolina in 1989, about a month before Hurricane Hugo came roaring through, she took up long-distance running as well.

Ironically, Hugo gave Wentworth a taste of the refugee experience. The storm's merciless 135 mile-per-hour winds left the Wentworth family homeless shortly after they'd moved into a quaint antebellum gate house on Sullivan's Island.

"I went from someone who had gone to graduate school in New York and been a very successful book publicist to having nothing. It is the worst thing that ever happened to me. Our house was destroyed. We lost everything we owned," Wentworth recalls. "We had never lived in a house before. It was gone in just a few hours. Thank God for friends and family who took us in. You do appreciate just having a normal life after that."

Many poems came out of the experience, words reflecting on the robust constitution of the Lowcountry landscape. "As we were trying to reconstruct our life, the land itself—the plants and landscape—we found to be quite resilient. It didn't take very long for the natural world to rebound. It's where great metaphors and symbols for strength and resurrection came from. I was just paying attention to what was around me."

Six white herons feeding at the edge of the pond.
I don't know what binds them to one another,
but their patience is certain. They came from a place
where bells mark the hour and nothing else

where time exists like a body of water
that stretches the reflection of a single pine tree
from one shore to another. And the ginkgoes
are always flaming at the water's edge.
      —from *Why I Run*

A chapbook, *Nightjars*, was published in 1995. All the while, Wentworth worked as a book publicist for other writers, and her husband continued his work attracting independent film-makers to the area.

In 2009, Wentworth published her first children's book, *Shackles*. It holds a special place in her heart because it is inspired by a true story in which her sons unearthed a pair of old slave shackles on the beach at Sullivan's Island. The story reflects on the painful history of America's slave trade. The book received the Silver Medal in the 2009 Moonbeam Children's Book Awards for multicultural children's publications.

The title of Wentworth's 2010 poetry collection, *The Endless Repetition of an Ordinary Miracle*, was pulled from a line in the novel *Snow* by Nobel Prize-winning Turkish author Orhan Pamuk. It celebrates the tiny, ordinary miracles that permeate everyday life. "In this book, I really wanted to celebrate little miracles," Wentworth explains. "I am actually a very happy person. I have a great life. I am not this dark, brooding, antisocial person."

On the cusp of a day, as birdsong
began braiding strands of sunlight
through night's raven hair
I took my first breath.
                    —from *Nightjars*

While teaching, Wentworth draws often on the wit and insight of her mentors in the master's program at NYU.

"Studying poetry in New York City is a quintessential creative experience, and I probably didn't realize how lucky I was at the time. The older I get and the more I write, the more grateful I am for the education I received there," Wentworth writes in her *Post and Courier* column in 2008. "I hear my teachers' voices in my head while I am writing. Little pearls of wisdom that have stayed in my brain, despite the passage of time, rise to the surface just when I need them most."

Wentworth's predominant go-to themes are resilience and the human spirit. "Like most people, I struggle with the most fundamental mysteries of experience: love and death," she told *The Post and Courier* in 2009. "Many of my poems are inspired by people who have literally survived the worse things that can happen to a human being."

In a 2012 interview with Kaite Hillenbrand with the online *Connotation Press*, Wentworth reflects on poetry's role in the lives of everyday people.

"Poetry is an unused resource, an art form that is too often overlooked and neglected. It is something we turn to in times of crisis, perhaps, but forget during the day-to-day rush of our lives. But isn't that when we need poetry more than ever?"

Danielle Howle

Musical Light

By Kyle Petersen

I often find it difficult to put into words the appeal of Danielle Howle. Calling her a singer-songwriter just doesn't fit; she's something more akin to a free-wandering spirit, an inquisitive mystic, or a hippie-beat poet, although none of those descriptions strikes the right chord either. Maybe it's best to start with her voice. It's a powerful and unique instrument that perpetually defies convention, whether she is singing country, jazz or rock and roll. The mixture of reference points seems endless. From the Indigo Girls, Kimya Dawson, and Patty Griffin to Janis Joplin, Sarah Vaughan, and Nina Simone, Howle definitively forges her own musical identity. What's more, she's a wild, oddly charismatic presence on stage, seeming both not of this world and all too human at the same time.

Talking to Howle is, in its own way, just as much of an experience as is seeing her perform. The first time I really got to talk to her—an interview at the rustic outpost in the Frances Marion National Park, where she is the artist-in-residence at a small, solar-powered studio—I got the sense that the singer was as close to an unvarnished, unfiltered human being as you can get. She's a wiry, free-spirited artist to her core. She punctuates the conversation with whoops, laughs, and (forgive the pun) howls, and it quickly becomes clear that the nervous, stream-of-conscious storytelling and odd asides that can bounce from brutally honest and tense to downright hilarious and joyous in a matter of moments during her performances is anything but an act. Howle is a live nerve of energy, emotion, and creativity, in a way that clearly explains from where the unique way she views the world in her lyrics comes. Our conversation bounces around from songwriting circles in Nashville and her recent show with the Avett Brothers to the recent protests over SOPA (the Stop Online Piracy Act) and the wily and (sometimes) wicked world of the music business, while various musicians and engineers drive up to the swamp house or stop to quickly ask a question or to give her a progress report on one project or another.

Since bringing the progressive rock act Lay Quiet Awhile to national (and international) attention in the early 1990s, Howle has recorded over a dozen full-lengths and EPs, often released by nationally recognized independent labels, and toured across the country time and time again with the likes of the Amy Ray, Elliott Smith, and Ani DiFranco. She's opened for acts as diverse as the Avett Brothers, Fugazi, Bob Dylan, and Hootie and the Blowfish. Her shifts in sound, style, and backing bands have pushed and pulled her categorization over the years, something which may cause marketing problems, but never stopped the singer herself. At the time of this writing, Howle had spent the last year playing out with The Firework Show, a new backing band which was named "Best

Experimental Band" in the Charleston City Paper. She's forward looking to a fault.

Still, the story of her journey over the years is a fascinating one. Born in Oklahoma to a military family which would move constantly, with time spent in Mississippi, Germany, and the Carolinas during her childhood, although "most of [that] was in the Columbia area," she says. And although she started playing in bands at 16, she's "been singing [her] whole life." After graduating Spring Valley High School, Howle came to town to attend Columbia College as a theater major. "That was the thing I loved [first]," she explains, and she credits her time there for helping her get more comfortable in her own skin. "I was really shy in a lot of ways, and it was a good place to not be…scared."

Howle first emerged on the Columbia music scene singing at open mics with a pick-up group called the Blue Laws and quickly drew a buzz due to her powerful and inventive voice, an odd instrument that sounded like nothing else at the time. From the beginning, she was a singular performer with a nervous energy and an in-the-moment charisma that carries her through her often rambling, stream-of-consciousness style. It was then that she started writing songs.

"I wrote in journals from third to tenth grade, and maybe that theater training brought me out of my shell a little bit—and I was about 21, and I was like, 'I think this is what I wanted to do,'" she recalls. Howle started learning how to play guitar and piano to accompany her burgeoning songwriting desire, and before long had built a strong reputation as a solo performer. What came next, though, is what shot Howle into national prominence.

Lay Quiet Awhile was a progressive-leaning college rock outfit that brothers Phil and Dan Cook started back in 1986. The brothers had gone through various line-up changes and recorded two EPs, but didn't really find their stride until Howle entered into the scenario. With Howle's quirky sensibilities and stop-you-in-your tracks voice, the band was clearly going places. Their inclusion on the 1992 WUSC fundraiser compilation Please No Profanity (which featured, among others, Hootie & the Blowfish, In/Humanity, and Blightobody), "Time Won't Help," became a staple in the station's rotation and built the group's reputation.

The band also would have a chance encounter with an unlikely supporter that would change the course of Howle's career—Indigo Girls' singer/songwriter Amy Ray. After picking up a last-minute gig opening for the Ellen James Society down in Charleston, and performing an inspiring opening set, Ray, who also runs the well-respected independent label, Daemon Records, which had Ellen James Society on their roster—approached the group and said, "'I want to sign you, do you know what I'm saying?' and I said, 'No, I don't!,'" Howle remembers with amusement.

Ray went on to release Lay Quiet Awhile's only full-length, 1993's *Delicate Wire*, and many other subsequent Howle releases, giving them great national exposure and an enhanced ability to tour nationally and in the UK. "I never would have been able to do anything without her. She's a great label boss and leader. She also trained me, by accident, to be a more socially conscious and politically conscious human being [as well], just by being who [she] was," Howle says.

Although *Delicate Wire* was the sole LP to come out of her days with Lay Quiet Awhile, in many ways it established the creative template for much of Howle's subsequent work. Many of the songs feature an echo of a folk tune they might have once been, but shifted and twisted through odd time signatures, propulsive rock and roll, and loose and limber jazz sensibilities.

After some lengthy touring, Lay Quiet Awhile called it quits—but Howle was just getting going. Soon after the group disbanded, Howle began collaborating with Blightobody guitarist John Furr on her solo record *About to Burst* (1996), beginning a musical relationship that would last well into the next decade. "John Furr is more talented and awesome than John Furr will ever realize," Howle still says proudly. "[and he's] rather unjaded and innocent about it."

As Danielle Howle & the Tantrums, Howle and Furr, along with drummer Troy Tague and bassist Brian Williams—would record two albums together, *Do a Two Stable* (1997) and *Skorborealis* (2002), both on Daemon, and tour across the country over the course of eight years. It was with the Tantrums that Howle was allowed to be her most willfully eclectic, going from country and Americana tunes and near-jazz standards to adrenaline-infused punk rock tunes and flight-of-fancy sonic experiments with a seamless ease, while also mixing a strong pop sensibility into the sound seemingly at will. Howle explains the differences between her two longest-running bands more in terms of feel than creative differences. "That's how I felt with those musicians [in Lay Quiet Awhile]—and I wasn't giving them a lot of my more Americana or country material."

During this time Howle also released two acoustic full-lengths, 1995's *Live at McKissick Stadium* (which featured acoustic versions of Tantrums songs) on Daemon and *Catalog* in 1999, which was released via the noted Pacific Northwest independent label Kill Rock Stars Records, the home or former home of such high-powered talent as Elliott Smith, The Decemberists, Sleater-Kinney, and Marnie Stern. Despite starting with limited instrumental skills, these records really demonstrated how Howle had fully assimilated the sensibilities of her full band arrangements into her own performance style. Although she had always played solo shows throughout her time with each band, she began spending more and more time on the road alone, guitar in hand, experiencing years of star-crossed adventures.

Gradually, the Tantrums became more of a casual, in-town band, particularly after *Skorborealis* came out in 2002, but luckily Howle still had yet even more musician-friends to help keep her relentless spout of songs going out to the public. This time, it was Hootie and the Blowfish's lead guitarist Mark Bryan who became her collaborator. Howle had known the band back when they were both in school in Columbia in the early 1990s—she had first met Bryan as a WUSC DJ, and became friends with the entire band once they started playing out live. "I use to hang out with Darius in his dorm room, just talking," she remembers, struck by how incongruous their fame and her memories are now. Of course, the band was also great fans of her work, and in 2005 Bryan produced and played on much of Howle's full-length *Thank You, Mark*, which Howle named in his honor. Rucker also contributed, singing a duet with her on the Etta James cover "If I Can't Have You."

The record found Howle working a more conventionally Americana mold, with tons of blues and jazz flourishes that played to one of the true strengths of the singer's inimitable voice. The polish and poise of the recording seemed to suggest that Howle might have another shot at mainstream success, with its readymade appeal to both the NPR and No Depression crowds. Still, although Howle toured heavily behind the record and won largely positive reviews, the momentum was difficult to maintain.

Howle had also begun doing various educational programming in 2001 as a way of making more money (as it turns out, being a full-time musician makes it difficult to pay the bills), running various programs at Penn State, College of Charleston, and other educational institutions throughout the Lowcountry and the Midlands. In 2006, she even penned a tune for ETV called "Wash Hands," which is now perhaps how she is best known to many parents in the state.

Still, the 2000s were often a struggle for Howle. She speaks bluntly about the waxing and waning of her financial success as a musician, noting in our interview that she "hadn't been to the doctor in 12 years" and that she "was still trying to figure out how to make a 'living wage' as a musician." Her life took another fortuitous turn, however, when she was made the artist-in-residence at Awendaw Green, a position which both gives her a place to live and a place to promote South Carolina artists at the Sewanee Outpost's weekly barn jams, as well as access to a solar powered swamp house (and makeshift recording studio) along the Echaw Creek deep in the Frances Marion Forest where our interview takes place. Howle got the gig through a friendship with Eddie White, who volunteered the swamp house to Howle at the end of 2008 for recording purposes, the results of which Howle released in 2009 as *The Swamp Sessions*. It is a rough-hewn acoustic record that was originally intended to be just a set of demos. "I made it in about six hours," she says almost apologetically. "It's really rough, but in a good way, I think."

That short, intimate experience sparked a much grander project that has become both Howle and Awendaw proprietor White's biggest passions—the next iteration of "The Swamp Sessions." Using Howle's long list of connections and talented friends, the two have orchestrated alchemic musical collaborations between an eclectic roster of South Carolina musicians, with enough songs recorded to fill out a 2-CD compilation. The long, impressive list of contributors includes, among others, Mark Bryan, Edwin McCain, Doug Jones, Cary

Ann Hearst, and Josh Roberts, as well as such unlikely contributors as poet laureate Marjorie Wentworth, saxophonist Charlton Singleton, and instrumentalist Dustin Ashenfelder. Almost all of the recordings feature Howle in some capacity, as well as the rhythm section of Firework Show.

And despite her long conversations frequent dwelling on the past, Howle is most excited when she talks about her new backing band, Firework Show, who back her on her newest full-length of original material, *New Years Revolutions.* The Charleston band formed in 2005 and had built a reputation for their extended jams that mixed psychedelia, blues, and jazz in a way not unlike Howle herself. Consisting of Zach Bodtorf (guitar/vocals), Brandon Gallagher (drums), Casey Atwater (bass), and Braxton Brown (keys), the group comes across as a looser, limber version of the Tantrums, and swings with as wild an eclecticism as Howle's oeuvre.

Despite a two decade reign as one of the state's leading musical lights, she's not anywhere near done. "I just keep following my muse until I find the next beautiful thing," she says. "It's gonna be a really interesting next 20 years."

Kay and Jim Thigpen

Theatre Heritage

By August Krickel

Columbia has always been a theatre town. No one is sure why, although some suspect that the numerous colleges and state government institutions ensure a relatively high level of literacy, and therefore appreciation of the arts. Others speculate that as the state capital, Columbia is a magnet for artistic folks from the hundreds of smaller, rural communities across the state who head to the big city for opportunity. City leaders often point to Jim and Kay Thigpen, the recently retired, iconic founders of Trustus Theatre as visionaries in the performing arts. In the mid-1980's, they saw a niche for progressive, alternative theatrical fare, the type being done in New York City, for example, took out a second mortgage on their home, and moved to an affordable area ripe for development, the warehouse district now called Columbia's Vista. By guaranteeing—and delivering—quality work, the Thigpens built a reputation that savvy audiences could trust—hence the catchy theatre name—and the fruit of their idea, work, and devotion grew into an acclaimed, professional regional theatre.

But many people don't realize that the Thigpens were working in the venerable tradition that stretches back nearly a century, past Kay's parents, Lou and Hazel Kaplan, to the years after the First World War. Many smaller Southern towns have what are often called *little theatres*, where amateur actors—those who perform on stage as a hobby or an avocation, rather than as a career—produce shows for friends and families. What makes Columbia different is that, in 1919, Daniel Reed was a captain stationed at *Camp* Jackson as the Army base was then known. A former professional Broadway actor before the war, Reed sensed an environment receptive to culture and performance, as there were already recitals, musical interludes, and readings from poetry and literature held in the auditorium of Columbia's only high school. Settling in town with his wife Isadora, Reed led the fledgling Columbia Stage Society to establish an actual theatre, located in an old house on Sumter Street, equidistant from the South Carolina State Capitol and the campus of the University of South Carolina. By late 1924, an actual theatre—the first designed specifically as a community theatre in the nation—was constructed; dubbed simply Town Theatre, the building remains the nation's oldest community theatre in continuous operation.

Conscious efforts were made to use all-local materials in the construction of the building, including bricks from Granby and fabric for the large stage curtain from the mill in Olympia. Reed served as resident director until 1927, and again from 1936 until 1938; local actors, directed by a professional, ensured quality and therefore popularity and success even during the lean years of the Depression and Second World War. The late Roy Mitchell, a long-time actor and board member at Town Theatre, recalled that in the 1940s and 50s, "we'd hire these young hotshots straight out of Yale Drama School. They'd work here for a year or two; build up some professional credits, and then move on to New York."

Two such hotshots were Fred Coe and Delbert Mann, who met at Vanderbilt University as undergrads, both later obtaining MFA's at Yale. Mann succeeded Coe as director at Town, and then followed him to New York, where both became successfully involved in live television drama. Mann's acclaimed production of *Marty* was expanded into a film version starring Ernest Borgnine, and was awarded multiple Oscars, including Mann as Best Director. In those years, a young USC student named Jasper Johns often volunteered to help paint sets, as did the teenage Christian Thee a decade later.

Lou Kaplan chose Columbia as the perfect spot to start his own business; having worked in the garment industry in New York City as a cutter, then designer of children's clothing, Kaplan moved south with his wife Hazel and daughter Kay, and opened the House of Fabrics in 1957. Kaplan had always been an avid lover and supporter of art, music and theatre. "My father fancied himself a writer," Kay Thigpen now recalls, and he penned skits for his children to perform at holiday gatherings.

Town Theatre soon came calling asking Kaplan to use his skills with fabric to help out as a costumer with theatre productions. His first acting role was in Arthur Miller's *A View from the Bridge*, performed at USC's Drayton Hall by the Hadassah Players, one of many civic and social clubs that also periodically mounted productions about town. Hazel Kaplan became a proficient make-up artist, and daughter Kay graduated from Columbia College with a degree in theatre, and taught in local high schools. Kay remembers enjoying her father in *Rashomon* the most, and also years later in *I'm Not Rappaport* at Trustus, the first time they were ever on stage together. As the city grew and young people everywhere sought to express themselves, the Kaplans joined some young Turks in 1967 to found Workshop Theatre, intended to open up directing and acting opportunities for a new generation, and to produce diverse and sometimes risky or cutting-edge theatrical works.

Still, their first production, *A Taste of Theatre*, consisted mainly of show tunes from popular favorites like *The King and I* and *Oliver!* The musical revue was performed at a small theatre on base at Fort Jackson. Kay Thigpen stage managed, and the show was co-directed by Jim E. Quick, who also dabbled in local television, appearing on a children's Saturday morning program as Chief Silly Horse. Quick appeared in *Dylan*, the first actual play Workshop produced, and he directed their second, *Peter Pan*, also performed at Fort Jackson. I sat in that audience as an eight-year-old fan of the Chief, but left as a fan of live theatre, marveling at the amazing simplicity of using a beam of light to represent Tinker Belle.

Jim Thigpen came to Columbia for graduate school in the 1970s, and stayed to teach high school. Before long he was a regular performer at Workshop Theatre, becoming their eventual board president during their first search for a permanent space. Then-City Councilman Kirkman Finlay, Jr. convinced him of the importance of the arts to the downtown area, and soon Workshop moved into and expanded on existing structures just off Gervais Street, adjacent to the Columbia Museum of Art. Jim met Kay when they were cast in a production of *Desire Under the Elms*, and they married in 1979. Lou had made his debut as director two years earlier with *The Glass Menagerie*, which was the first play that I ever went to see of my own accord—not taken by an adult or as part of a school trip, in other words. Purchasing my own ticket with money that I had earned, choosing my preferred destination for entertainment, and having already read the material, I imagined myself to be a cosmopolitan theatre-goer. Jim wasn't in the cast, but his face was borrowed for a stage prop, a photo of the play's absentee father. Ever the entrepreneur, Lou was later involved with a number of subsequent start-up theatre groups, including several attempts at dinner theatre.

After a grant from the National Endowment for the Humanities allowed Jim to study contemporary theatre for a summer in New York City, he and Kay realized that there were dozens of edgy, ambitious new plays not being done in Columbia, despite the considerable local talent and resources available to do small-cast, one-set shows. Columbia is a theatre town, but each theatre group had a core mission and catered to specific demographics. Newer plays, lesser-known plays, and especially plays with mature themes or language were rarely produced.

In 1985, the Thigpens opened their 50-seat theatre in an upstairs space on Assembly Street, surrounded then as now by pawn shops. «We were the theatre that curses, and does nude shows,» Jim often jokes, but they also served beer, wine, and popcorn, hoping to establish a cozy, welcoming environment. Lou turned up in character roles until he was nearly 90 years old. Relocating to their current location on Lady Street in 1988, Trustus pioneered the rebirth of the surrounding area as an arts district. They were the Vista before the Vista was cool. Now in its 28th season, Trustus continues to garner critical acclaim, often hosting the regional premieres of award-winning shows from Broadway and beyond. Their acclaimed Playwrights› Festival, started in 1989, allows exposure for new playwrights via a professional production of their work. David Lindsay-Abaire, the Festival winner in 1995 for *A Show of Hands*, went on to win the Pulitzer Prize in 2007 for *Rabbit Hole*, which Trustus then produced the following year with Kay Thigpen and Vicky Saye Henderson in in the cast. In addition to a full season of full-scale productions, Trustus also offers smaller shows in an intimate black box setting and an off-site series of productions, as well as late night entertainment, acting classes, a teen Apprentice Company, and a Multi-Ethnic Acting Workshop, which has in turn led to a spin-off group, the NiA Company.

The last Trustus show in the old Assembly Street location, *The Woolgatherer*, was a two-character play featuring just Jim and Kay; I reviewed that show for the brand new alt-paper *Free Times*, and turned my copy into my arts editor a few days later. Also an actress and dancer, she appeared in *Hair*, the first production at the new Trustus location. I missed that performance because I was in rehearsals at Town Theatre for *The Magnificent Yankee*, a bio of Oliver Wendell Holmes, sponsored by the South Carolina Bar as part of a series of plays dealing with Constitutional issues, commemorating the 200th anniversary of its signing. A guest director was brought in: Delbert Mann, returning to the site of his first professional gig to direct one last show. One of the cast members became my roommate; two years later, I was playing Lou Kaplan's grandson in *Broadway Bound* at Town Theatre, and the roommate and the editor were engaged. Fast forward another 21 years, and their son is now a regular in shows at the Village Square Theatre in Lexington. Local theatre is like that: one connection leads to another, and just about everything comes full circle. Actors so often marry other actors, since rehearsal is the only place they ever go; children see their parents or neighbors on stage, and in every audience, there's a boy or girl silently thinking "I can *do* that. I've *got* to do that."

Kay Thigpen notes that young, talented performers find Columbia to be an incredibly nurturing and supportive environment, but often want to seek their fortunes elsewhere, "to go and try, and see how they stack up against everyone else. And they may be as good or better than anyone else, but discover that it's not necessarily just about talent." And so they may return to Columbia, happy to earn a living wage, and perhaps start a career or family ... yet as soon as that dream role comes open, the acting bug will bite again. Jim and Kay both acknowledge that a dedicated performer will go anywhere for a role, paid or not, and give a professional performance. This may explain in part why there is so much theatre in Columbia, so much good theatre, and so many good people involved. Sandra Willis and Jeni McCaughan, the current executive directors at Town and Workshop Theatres, echo this sentiment, agreeing that "actors will come out of the woodwork" when a popular show is announced.

Jim and Kay Thigpen are now happily retired grandparents, but still Trustus board members *emeritus*, and the main stage now bears the name Thigpen; a photo portrait of Lou Kaplan hangs in the lobby, while just a few miles away, Workshop's downstairs makeup/dressing room bears Hazel Kaplan's name.

I still have fond memories of playing Roy Mitchell's nephew in the first community theatre show I did locally, as well as being directed by Jim E. Quick in his last. Larry Hembree and Dewey Scott-Wiley, veteran stage directors, actors, and professional arts administrators, now share leadership at Trustus in its 28th season; Workshop marks its 45th anniversary this year, while Town is in its 93rd year. Columbia's theatre roots may have started with amateurs in that word's truest sense—a *lover* of theatre, compensated by the intangible—but a populace receptive to performing arts was willing to recruit and support professionals, who often went on to national acclaim.

Entrepreneurs began to expand the number of venues, their children became teachers, and yet another generation became trained theatre professionals and community leaders. In addition to colleges and the three main community theatres detailed above, there are at least eight other groups producing shows in borrowed, refurbished or adapted spaces across the Midlands, from Forest Acres to Chapin to Lexington. Simply put, Columbia is a theatre town. Live theatre, done locally but with professional quality and production values, has been a collective vision shared across the last century by the Reeds, the Kaplans, the Thigpens, and the entire arts community, a vision that we continue to benefit from today.

Nikky Finney

Poet of Action

"She would rather be the one deciding what she keeps and what she throws away."

By Colena Corbett

The craft of writing is a thoughtful art that happens daily as we move. Every action creates a string of ideas and impulses. Throughout our movement there can be a sea of metaphors: stifling briars, and on one end the pastoral scene of red clover and jasmine; there are traces of saltwater and the sounds of freeness; there are collections of the mechanical music on urban streets; and there are the words that stir inside of you as you swallow them. As we live, one is still listening, paying attention, doing the work required. This comes through the reading we take in and from the experiences we've encountered along the way. "I simply fell in line where I was needed" (Ambrosia 144). That line from Nikky Finney's essay "Ambrosia" I read reinvigorated me, as I was learning how to navigate a path while working in the world. Crafting out a plan is a conscious decision of what we will sacrifice and what we will choose to keep. I was a woman making choices which many close to me did not understand. What I've realized was that I was never alone.

I had just returned from a women writers' workshop in Lexington, Kentucky in the middle of May. In this workshop I was talking with writers, thinkers, scholars, and independent musicians; women of various ages who were creating their paths, while some already there, were discussing their current roles in their very rich lives. A community was being constructed there in those blue hills over the weekend, some educated, some self-taught, all writers; and I met women I would stay connected to for the remainder of my life. I learned that one young woman in this same workshop was headed to another writing program in New England—the same one I was headed to in a few weeks—so we remained in contact the weeks prior to leaving our homes and during our stay up north. It was one of the most meaningful times in my life —that weekend in Kentucky, listening in that library space, sitting on the warm concrete at the Northside Branch Library.

Nikky Finney and her colleague, Dr. Melynda Price, planned the workshop based on Finney's own early experience with mentor Toni Cade Bambara in Atlanta. I was extremely excited, nervous, and grateful. I knew opportunities like this did not come every day. This weekend with Nikky Finney only required that the members bring mindfulness—and that we bring someone with us; we were to share our experience with someone else.

On the first night, the workshop group was assigned to read Toni Cade Bambara's essay "The

Education of A Storyteller." This piece, Finney explained, was one of her *writerly* maps. As we discussed Bambara's work, we focused so much on the stories of our elders and how these stories return to us as we are learning new philosophies and theories as students and readers. As we accumulate new knowledge from the world, our histories and lessons from our elders must be respected and acknowledged (Bambara 250).

My spirit was full. And upon my return home to North Carolina I had to go see my 80-year-old neighbor and tell her about what happened that weekend. In Kentucky the space was not about one person in particular; we all had various projects we were pursuing at the time; we all had parts to play. We were coalescing; and we were pushing each other to do the work required of us. My neighbor smiled in her robe as she was searching through sheets of papers, "Here, I think you can use this. I've got more on the history, if I look in that box."

Nikky Finney, I believe, is a woman who values the minds of people, their stories, their communities, and their families. She is always teaching—even when she goes out for ice at the local store; she talks to neighbors; she talks to people walking at stoplights. She is also very passionate and serious about the lives she touches. She reminds people that their words do matter and she holds us accountable for what we write.

Nikky Finney has written four books of poetry: *On Wings Made of Gauze* (1985); *Rice* (1995); *The World Is Round* (2003); and *Head Off & Split* (2011), which won the National Book Award. She has also written a book of interrelated short-stories called *Heartwood* (1998). In her collections of poetry, Finney shares the personal and sometimes painful histories of her family, her take on American history, her passion for nature, her sexuality, and her readings from newspapers and popular science magazines. Finney, in her crafting of theme, tells stories that are linked and takes many risks in her own work. Within her signature word creations, her gripping persona poems, and her love for the epigraph, she is teaching poets even as they read to do more than write, and that is to follow motivation with action. Finney was taught this idea while she was finding her *writerly* plan after leaving Talladega College for Atlanta, Georgia.

Finney found living examples of people of action beginning with her activist parents, her grandmother, her college teacher, Dr. Gloria Wade Gayles, and her mentor, writer Toni Cade Bambara. She witnessed Bambara's activism in her writings, as well as her life ("Ambrosia" 142-151). Under Toni Cade Bambara, Finney observed intergenerational learning encounters within the community where Bambara lived. There is a mutual experience that can happen between generations; they have something powerful to take away from a moment in learning together. Finney's work is paying attention to the lessons from her grandmother, Beulah Davenport; but not only that, Finney's work studies the people that may have been overlooked; she tells the stories that are not told.

In her prose poem "Hurricane Beulah" Finney writes "Every time I ask her does she need my help she sucks her teeth real loud and moves on up the aisle away from me, blues singing something about, 'Don't treat me like I am old, treat me like I can be recycled, remember'" (TWIR 40). As a woman who is concerned about the environment, Finney gives her readers such richness in her language. Not only does she make a conscious effort to discuss the issue of conservation of resources, she also makes a point in this prose selection to save people—those walking libraries around us. In our workshop discussion on Bambara's essay Finney explained that we must not only share the new knowledge that we come across, but we must come back—to our homes, where we left— to share it with the ones who taught us first; we must never forget those early lessons and the history that some were trained to forget. Those individuals who never had the opportunity to learn, we cannot forget their contributions to us arriving to this point. Finney explained that sometimes, "...our elders have been taught that they have to teach younger ones something else in order to assimilate... and forget all of that other stuff [we] learned at home." She feels this disconnect between generations is something that she could not grasp and it was often hard to witness when observing the younger generations of writers and artists.

In her 2003 book *The World Is Round* her poem "Fishing Among the Learned" explores her first educational encounters surrounded in nature "staring up at this Human University" (101). She is encouraged to listen, to take what she needs, and to always put back (102). She has followed this practice because she's had teachers who have used this same pedagogy with her.

In reading Finney's work, not only is there pedagogy but process. I have shared with her that I have seen the images of cutting-away, or the decision of what to save and what to keep throughout her work; this for me equates the decision of the writing process. I remembered it vividly in reading "Hurricane Beulah" where grandmother Beulah asks Finney if she has been watching closely and learning about what must be kept, what can be recycled, and what can be discarded (42). This same image or reference to a woman's decision of what she keeps or saves can be read in the beginning of her book *Head Off & Split* in "Resurrection of the Errand Girl: An Introduction." Finney begins with the poet/speaker's decision about what she keeps, because she is a "Girl no longer girl" (3). She "understands/ sharpness & duty. She knows what a blade can reveal & destroy" (3). In the lines from "Penguin, Mullet, Bread" Finney's mother has kept her away "from sharp things that might/slip into [her] throat and never completely/ disappear" (83). Finney very early understood human responsibility and work, and discipline, and how it impacts those around you. That when you grow, you take on more and have the autonomy to exercise that freedom to save a life.

"Red Velvet," another poem, retells the history of Rosa Parks, but it also conveys a parallel theme. What is unique is not Finney's characterization of Parks, but the juxtaposition of the early events during the Civil Rights Movement paired with Park's own images of (cutting) crafting hand made things, next to her crafting out a plan for her activism:

Arching herself over a river of cloth she feels for the bias,

but doesn't cut, not until the straight pins are in place,

marking everything; in time, everything will come together.

Nine months after, December 1, 1955, Claudette

Colvin, fifteen, arrested for keeping her seat; before that,

Mary Louise Smith. The time to act, held by two pins.

—from *Head Off & Split*

Rosa Parks acts because she must, but first she plans it out, she studies, she's careful. She is a "woman who believes she is worthy of everything possible" (11). Parks is doing the work that is required of her, thus changes lives in the process.

In that final night of that Kentucky workshop the members in that small group were sharing books, discussing their writing, and offering their lives as teachable moments. All of these ideas are present memory as I am going home so full after a good meal, but I don't go to sleep at the wheel. I think about the stories I have heard from the women in my family, the stories I've read, the people I've encountered. They all serve as an impetus for my direction.

All of these stories are what makes me excited about writing; I look at the people who have faced great challenges—the ones who have looked their fears straight in the eye and kept it moving. That's what good teaching does; it allows you to bring things together in order to visualize a larger tapestry that can be enjoyed. Nikky Finney's poems and essays do more than just teach, they serve as a reminder of what writing has done and what it will do to those who read it with desire. It encourages generations to revisit and explore history together. It encourages the study of language and the mastery of revision; it invites; it coalesces and teaches beyond those long, fluid, engaging poetic lines that draw us in like a sleeping new baby's eye lashes. Each time we go back to look we see something we didn't notice before happening.

Notes

Finney, Nikky. *The World Is Round.* Atlanta, GA: Innerlight Publishing, 2003.

---.*Head Off & Split.* Evanston, Il: TriQuarterly Books/ Northwestern P, 2011.

---."Ambrosia" *Shaping Memories, Reflections of African American Women Writers.* Ed. Joanne

Veal Gabbin. Jackson, MS: University of Mississippi P, 2009.

Bambara, Toni Cade. "The Education of a Storyteller." *Deep Sightings & Rescue Missions,*

Fiction, Essays, & Conversations. Ed. Toni Morrison. New York, NY.

Stephen Chesley

Artist and Mentor

By Susan Lenz

Bastille Day 2001, personal date of independence. I fire my head mat cutter and cannot do his work and mine; the two jobs total twenty-five hours per day. My custom picture framing business must be forcibly downsized. I must admit the reason for such a drastic action: I want to be an artist.

This is ridiculous, of course. I have no training, no experience, and no academic background. My last art class was in the eighth grade. I don't even paint. There's just this silly notion, a dream. Maybe, just maybe ... pulling thread through fabric might constitute art making.

No one kills a wildly successful business for a pipe dream. Art is a fantasy and I must be crazy. People will undoubtedly laugh. Others will think me more insane than ever before. I need someone to talk to. I need advice, a sounding board, direction, hope ... I need a mentor.

On Monday morning, my utility van almost drives itself to Prentice Avenue, the home of a client, a self-supporting landscape oil painter, Stephen Chesley.

Stephen Chesley has talent in spades. His brushstrokes tell stories of atmospheric conditions on sun soaked afternoons and fire fly evenings. Smoke vapors rise from red primed surfaces and reflections of dawn ripple across inlet coves. Chesley's oils are magic. Chesley's pastels ooze with the sensation of mud between barefoot toes that creep across relic sand on twilight beaches. He is an artist, the kind of artist I longed to be.

He made tea. I cried self-pitying tears of fear and doubt. What would he think of this hair-brained idea of mine ... me, setting off to be an artist, thinking I might one day be a peer, gambling with my family's entire income, doing something totally irrational?

"I want to be an artist."

"You already are one. Now ... just go do the work."

For two hours the conversation meandered through the details of a creative existence. He talked about juried exhibitions, portfolios, resumes, labeling slides, charity events, daily commitment, greed, talent, skill, gallery representation, and how to keep an inventory book. He never laughed. Lastly, he reiterated, "Now ... just go do the work."

The van seemed to know its way back home. Good thing. My mind wasn't on the traffic. It was trying to absorb more practical information than most studio art majors hear in four years of college. Chesley promised that a career in art was simple. He said, "Here's a pencil. Here's a piece of paper. All you have to do is go out and make a living." He wasn't trying to change my mind. None of his statements were issued as a warning. He knew just what to say and how to say it ... straightforward, almost blunt, and totally honest. "Now ... just go do the work."

No one said it would be easy. Chesley certainly didn't suggest a painless path. I got a studio and an ordinary accountant's ledger to track my progress, my finished pieces ... just as he'd advised. I went to work. What did Chesley say? "Only you can make an original Susan Lenz. Now ... just go do the work"

When I complained, he had a suggestion. "Make a series ... one hundred pieces. Explore every possibility. Make sure the last one is as fresh, spontaneous, and full of life as the first had been." Chesley knew what he was talking about. He knew the dedication and challenge such an adventure requires. He understood the growth an artist experiences while creating one hundred related pieces. More than an exercise, Chesley's proposition implied deeper concepts and a richly saturated journey. He'd been down this path before and I knew it. I'd seen and framed his series, *107 Ordinary Days*.

During the first half of the year 2000 Stephen Chesley created one hundred and seven consecutive drawings in as many days, graphite on toned paper with China white highlights. I framed them; he crated them. A decade went by until they emerged as an October exhibit at Gallery 80808 in the Vista, Columbia's arts and cultural district. Chesley called the works "timepieces," fresh and new, from a long gone day and an imaginary place. They are back in their crates again. Viewing is only possible via an unbound mind … until 2020.

During that same month, my *Decision Portraits*, a series of quilts depicting a variety of individuals and the decisions they made, both profound and run-of-the-mill, were on view in City Gallery at Waterfront Park in Charleston. I don't know how it happened. It certainly wasn't intentional but there are exactly one hundred and seven pieces in that series. Good number. Good advice.

By this time, Chesley had moved into a rental space at Vista Studios. It is literally across the hallway from my studio. Good advice floats over the partition walls with the steady stream of artists seeking counsel. Some don't even know they're looking for direction. They think they're just visiting, having an idle conversation, talking about mutual concerns or complaining about the economy. Supposed chitchat, but not really.

They leave after a creative alignment. They leave after conversations about pricing or the bare bone facts on taxes or artistic investments or the power found in hours of drawing and weeks of historic research. They leave with a final statement from an ultimate mentor, "Now … just go do the work."

I've overheard frequent discussions about artistic influences … a Who's Who exchange of A-list names … Innes, Homer, Whistler, Hopper, Ryder, Gauguin, Turner, Kline. But, Chesley is wise. He listens until he can calmly explain by example, knowing how to translate inspiration from others into very personal explorations; the sort of work that remains true to his individual voice.

After seeing *Turner to Cezanne: Masterpieces from the Davies Collection, National Museum Wales* at the Columbia Museum of Art in 2009, Chesley was profoundly struck by the lone Vincent Van Gogh piece on view, *Landscape at Auvers in the Rain*. He knew the masterpiece was painted less than two weeks before Van Gogh took his own life. He also knew how to take such powerful emotions and influential desires and make them his own.

Research. Contemplation. Adaptation.

Chesley learned that Van Gogh created twenty-three works in July 1890 ... before the 27th day, his last. He researched the sizes to the inch and built stretcher bars to the same dimensions. He pulled and stapled linen and primed the surfaces. Then, on July 1st, Chesley immersed himself in a parallel endeavor, a physical challenge to address painting as Van Gogh had done; to work through inclement weather, to load his brush and twist paint into lunar orbs against starry nighttime skies. Chesley pushed through the demands of long hours in order to achieve the same square inches of perfection as Van Gogh had done. He quit on July 27th. Inspiration became an experience.

Chesley exhibited *27 Days in July* later that same year. It was a perfect example of artistic influence without sacrificing personal stylistic choices, without stealing content or meaning, without compromise. "Now ... just go do the work." Chesley did. He still does, every day, day after day.

Productivity can be assumed when one is living such a creative, professional artistic life. Chesley's studio is a maze of oils on panel, piles of sketches, stretched linen canvases stacked against metal sculptures, reference books mingled between folders of pastels, and frames in various conditions. (The frames were all perfect when I delivered them. Cramped conditions and the constant arrangements result in too many nicks and bumps.) How does he keep track?

Well, there's a series of inventory books. On my very first day of being an artist Chesley instructed me to keep one, too. They are just ordinary accountants' ledgers. Each finished piece is listed beside a thumbnail sketch. Next are the dimensions, media, completion date, notations on anything special or unusual, price, and an inventory number. Hopefully, several of the entries will later come to include a buyer's name and contact information. My last number in my inventory book is #1819. Chesley's listings have five digits.

A couple of years ago, my husband Steve and I went to the National Gallery of Art to see the Edward Hopper retrospective. It was wonderful, of course. We wandered from room to room trying not to become overwhelmed until we nearly bumped into a large, Plexiglas covered pedestal. Inside were Hopper's inventory books, each with a thumbnail sketch, dimensions, media, completion date, notations, price, and an occasional buyer's name. I was stunned.

Within the week, I told Chesley about the show and the inventory books. He laughed. "I thought I told you!" he said. "I've always kept such an inventory book because, well, if it was good enough for Hopper, it was good enough for me." Funny thing is, I've always kept such an inventory book because if it was good enough for Chesley, it was good enough for me.

It's been just over eleven years since I started that inventory book. I've grown to be a professional studio artist, the kind I longed to be. I was lucky in many respects but there wasn't luck involved in the advice received; just truth, brutal and honest. I still struggle with too many moments of doubt, pitiful emotions, and issues of low self-esteem. Chesley occasionally has to roll his eyes at me, but he does so with a smile. He knows I know what to do.

"Now ... just go do the work".

Philip Mullen

Dialogue Artist

By Cassie Premo Steele

During a time of stuckness, the kind of inertia that many creative people occasionally endure, I had started going to a yoga center regularly, and the physical movement allowed a creative movement within me to begin again. Wanting something deeper than I could, at the time, express through language, I had begun to paint.

Summer turned to fall, and the yoga center had a one-year celebration and asked me to compose an anniversary poem and display a few of my paintings. During the evening's festivities, a tall, professorial-looking man who taught yoga classes at the center came up and commented on one of my paintings.

"I think I've seen that before," he said.

A bit fearful that he was criticizing my work, I quipped, "Only if you've been in my bedroom recently!"

His bright blue eyes flashed, and he laughed. A friendship was born.

Later, someone told me who he was: Philip Mullen, one of South Carolina's greatest painters, whose huge works honor the walls of the University of South Carolina's Koger Center for the Arts, whose work has been exhibited in the

Whitney Museum, the Brooklyn Museum, and Smithsonian, and whose prolific career includes thirty-one years as a professor of art at the University of South Carolina, from which he retired as Distinguished Professor Emeritus in 2000.

But this is not how I met him. When I met him, I used the label, "yoga teacher" in my mind. When he met me, he used the label, "aspiring artist" in his. In this way, our friendship was born out of illusion—and out of the truth that depth does not come from surfaces or labels or the first impressions we get from the social exterior. He had turned to yoga after having to leave tennis; I turned to painting during a time when words were failing me. Interestingly, our friendship was born in a context of change and loss. These, I would discover, are also major themes in Philip Mullen's work.

———

One spring, I went to see the Philip Mullen 1994-2008 Exhibit at the Sumter County Gallery of Art. While there, I saw Booth Chilcutt, and told him how much I loved Philip's work. Booth asked me if I'd like to do a writing workshop in conjunction with the show. I said yes. Booth did not know that I knew Philip, and Philip found it funny that fate had brought us together in yet another unexpected context.

As I prepared for the workshop, I wrote several poems in response to his work. At the workshop, I read the poems, and then asked participants to write their own. I did not know it then, but

I was engaging in what Philip has called "dialogue." It is his term for how he wants the viewer to engage in the paintings—not as an object, but as a subject that speaks and asks the viewer to speak, as well. Here is one of the poems I wrote:

As the Image Moves through Light

"Acquire a method for contemplating how all things are transformed into one another. Observe each thing, and imagine that it is in the process of dissolving, that it is in the midst of transformation, in the process of putrefying and being destroyed."

Marcus Aurelius

There are walls that wave like water

and windows in the midday sun.

A series can only begin to say it.

All through the beginning of that year,

there are times that color

could choke you with its beauty.

For hours you would stare

at one vase—

but there is not enough time

-- and there is never one place.

As the image moves through light,

you must trace

them over and over again.

Life is like that

in its too muchness.

Walls. Windows. Corners. Sun.

You fill the vase again and again,

and yet it seems you've only just begun.

———

After the workshop, Philip told me that hearing my poems and writing his own in response to his painting allowed him to see his paintings in a new way. This surprised me, his humbleness and openness to seeing his art, not as a static object somehow removed from everyday human life, but as a living thing. As a partner in a relationship.

A few months later, we both decided we wanted to attend a weekend of yoga workshops in Asheville, and he offered to drive me there and back. The classes were fine, the meals we shared even finer, but what I remember most were the conversations we had on the drive.

We had moved, in our friendship, from first impressions to a mutual recognition of each other's work, and now we were entering new territory. As the mountains grew up around us on the drive, I remember feeling that it was the two of us who were going deeper, into a place where artists share the deepest thoughts about their work and lives.

At one point, I told him that I sometimes doubt myself—my work, the impact of my writing on the world.

"Have you ever read a poem that touched you so deeply that you were grateful to be alive?" he asked me.

"Yes," I said. "Of course."

"Then you can be sure that someone out there has read one of your poems and felt the same."

It stunned me—the simplicity of it. The generosity of it. The sense that we are all here, as humans, as creative beings, giving our work to others, and being grateful for each other's work.

And that when we are aware of the shared mutuality of this, the fears can begin to fall away.

I was also launching my new business as a creativity coach at the time, after many years of teaching as an adjunct at the university. Philip's advice to spend half my time on writing and half my time on business freed me. It allowed me to view both my writing and my coaching as part of this generous service to others that he had modeled to me.

One fall, I decided to organize a series of Co-Creating workshops, inviting guest artists to share their work and give people opportunities to engage—as we did in the Sumter exhibit—with the work in their own personal ways. Philip agreed to be the first guest artist for the series, and he planned to bring his new paintings that he called "Praises."

As we sat outside at a coffee shop and discussed our ideas for the workshop, I said to him, "In your paintings, things are not things."

He smiled and said, "That is one of the nicest things anyone has ever said to me. Tell me more."

"Well, you call it dialogue, but there's more to it than that. It's that the objects themselves in the paintings change—with the light, with the space, with the relationship to the other elements in the painting—and they reveal their aliveness. It makes the viewer realize art is not just a thing—and that we are not things, either—that everything is alive and changing, has a history, a depth, and an emotional life."

"Yes," he said. "That's it. In paintings, things are not things."

Philip and I once gave back-to-back talks at May Carolina, an event organized by the University of South Carolina Alumni Association, and I began to see this idea of "a thing is not a thing" in a new light.

In his talk at May Carolina, he showed slides of how this works. The fascinating thing about his process is that he paints over previously completed—and shown—paintings in creating new ones. In slide after slide, he showed paintings that were beautiful, completed, finished—and yet layered over to become wholly new. It is the layering of the past—how the depth of history comes through the painting—in color and form and texture that intrigues him.

It is the way a friendship begins with a surface image but only develops over time and layers of emotional depth.

While Philip has had great success with figurative paintings over the course of his career, his work has become increasingly abstract, in the sense that even the objects in the paintings are both there and not there.

I recently met Philip for lunch and an afternoon

of visiting his studio, and was struck by how his newest works seem to go from meditations on light into a wetness, a drowning, in watery space.

I asked him about this. "Is it the final form—the depth and layering—that matters most to you? Or the emotional unfolding over time?"

"Both," he said. "I don't talk about the emotions very much, but they are there."

"So, when you paint over the women, over the men, over the figures, are you reflecting on destruction? On mortality and loss? A kind of mandala-like wiping away of the creation?"

"No," he said. "They are all still there. I don't see it as destruction but a kind of insistence on creation, on the movement of creation into greater depth and space."

I thought about those moments in a life when everything falls apart—and yet somehow you move on. "It's the way," I said, "Creatively and in life itself, we find ways to keep going, to go to a new place, to create a new life, and eventually we look back and it's not even that we can say we regret the past."

"Yes," he said. "Because it's all still there. It's what's underneath. It's what creates the depth."

I looked at the white space, the openness, in his paintings, how each is as large, spatially and emotionally, as a room. And because I had seen the slides of these same paintings from earlier incarnations, I thought about the years—the meticulous work, the figures, the drawings, even the emotional work of having shown them previously—and it struck me as incredibly courageous. To let all this go.

―

"Let's talk about work," I said.

"Okay."

"You and I both teach that you can't plan the work, that it isn't something that can be worked out ahead of time."

"Right. You know, people come up to me all the time and say, 'I've got all these great ideas. I just can't seem to get them out on paper.'"

"Right," I said. "It's like when people say to me that they are going to write a book one day and I say, writing only happens when you're writing."

He nodded. "A painting is not an idea."

"A book is not an idea," I said.

I looked around the room at the dozens of paintings in the studio, dozens more in the storage room, dozens and dozens more in galleries and museums and private collections—and thought about how each one represented not just one painting, but many.

"Creating is not an idea," I said. "But that's not to say it isn't work, either. The work takes a long time. You've taught me that. I used to think a book was done, but knowing you has taught me that when I think it is done, it usually needs four more years of layering, of depth, of revision."

"Right."

"So how does this go along with the idea that it can't be planned?" I asked.

"You commit to the work. You do the work," he said. "You prepare. You have discipline. And once you are in the space of the work, that's when you let go."

My eyes widened. I looked around the room at the space within each painting. "The paintings are about letting go into a new space just as the creative process itself is a letting go into the new!" I exclaimed.

"Right, that's right."

"And yet it doesn't happen all at once," I said. "I have clients who come to me and say, 'I want to write something positive, I want to enrich the world,' so I say to them, 'That only happens after you've walked through the shadow, after you've put words on what has brought you here.'"

"Exactly," he smiled. "These paintings are what they are because of what they have been."

"And the open space, the sense of freedom and possibility," I continued. "This is only possible with the depth. It comes about as a result of facing the history, coming to terms with the figures underneath and that past?"

"Perfect."

———

The next day, he called me to say he couldn't sleep the night before and started the new book I'd given him, currently being considered by an editor at a press. He told me he couldn't put it down and read 88 pages before going back to bed.

"It's the creative process that you capture so exactly," he said. "How you say most people start with the classes—the technique, the practice of learning how to do something as someone else has done it, and they never leave that—they never take that leap to begin for themselves."

"It's like a hamster wheel," I said. "They keep going around and around instead of jumping from the trapeze."

"I like that," he said.

"I think I just got the ending image for the essay," I told him.

"See?" he laughed. "You couldn't plan that!"

"And yet," I said. "You've taught me to be doing the work so that when the unplanned happens, you are ready for it."

"You're ready," he said.

"Thank you for helping to teach me to be ready."

"You're welcome," he said. And in his words, there was such depth that it was easy to get back to work.

Robert Richmond

Bravery

By Chad Henderson

Columbia theatre is embarrassingly rich by having Robert Richmond in its midst. He's directed productions that have appeared Off-Broadway and at La Jolla Playhouse, and he helmed over a dozen shows with Aquila Theatre's National Tours. He also directed a production of *Much Ado About Nothing* which was performed at a private reception for the President in 2005 at the White House (yeah, *that* President). Now Richmond is a professor with the Theatre and Dance Department at the University of South Carolina, and his shows have broken some of the University's theatre attendance records. In his time as a professor he's also directed a production of *Othello* at the Folger Theatre in Washington, DC—which won the coveted Helen Hayes Award. To say that this man has influenced me would be an understatement: he has inspired me.

Richmond has been a mentor and friend to this young theatre director ever since we met—and I'm eternally grateful. I met Richmond when I was in college, but I was never a student there while he was a professor. His mentorship has existed through conversations, philosophizing, and support—a sort of unofficial education accrued over coffee and having the chance to watch him work.

My first directing mentor in college was Karla Koskinen. She taught directing to the undergraduates at Theatre South Carolina, and she allowed me to do an independent study with her. She also served as my Honors Senior Thesis advisor. She laid the groundwork for the start of my career by giving me the tools to approach and analyze a script; to find out WHAT the play was saying and WHY it was saying it. I hadn't met Robert Richmond yet – but for me, he would be instrumental in unlocking the HOW.

I probably met Richmond at the auditions for *As You Like It* which Theatre South Carolina was producing at the end of my senior year in college, but I definitely remember meeting him during the first rehearsal for the show in which I was cast as William. Earlier in my college career I had the misfortune of being cast in another guest director's production. I won't say his name—but I felt like he hated our guts. This director was *tired*, his show was *tired*, and we were all *tired* of being in it—basically, it was one of those "eat shit and grin" situations. Consequently, I didn't have any expectations going into my first rehearsal for *As You Like It*.

As I sat in that first rehearsal, I took a look at the man who was directing the show. He was British, that much was certain. But at that time he was a New Yorker who wore bright colored polo shirts with the collar popped, and sported a clean-as-a-whistle bald head. He certainly looked cool to this impressionable youth who was used to the more formal—academic look of the rest of the faculty.

Richmond was quick and to-the-point in that rehearsal, and when he asked questions of us he wanted the visceral answer. Something about the way he was working made immediate sense to me. We went on in that rehearsal to dance in a circle, roamed the rehearsal space as different zoo animals, and performed a multitude of other exercises which seemed totally unrelated to the task of acting this Shakespearean piece.

As rehearsals continued throughout the week, I realized that all of these exercises were making us uninhibited as a cast. We had done thoroughly embarrassing things in front of each other, and made total fools of ourselves—but now we were willing to *try anything*. We also started picking up on each other's rhythms and working better as a collective.

Now—let me say that *this specific* week alone has proven extremely pivotal in my work as a professional director. What I watched Robert do that week was tear down our little walls that we all keep up. For actors, it's often times hard to incite vulnerability. When you're out on stage, you want—for some understandable but unnecessary reason—to be *liked* by the audience. So it feels safe to go out there and "put on a show" – almost like you and the audience are the only ones working together.

But take a moment and consider the performances that have moved and engaged you while watching a play. I'll bet you felt that way because you BELIEVED the actors; they were telling the truth on stage. To do this requires some vulnerability, and to be effectively vulnerable as an actor you must be able to trust yourself and your fellow cast-mates.

This brings me back to this week of exercises I was going on about before: those exercises had built an ensemble. I hadn't had the light bulb moment in my career yet where I knew that directing a trusting ensemble was a vital step in creating an effective theatrical story—but the seed was planted that week and it has grown over the years into process and philosophy for me.

As the process went on with Richmond, we started to form a relationship that I've valued every day since. I instantly took an interest in him and for whatever reason—he took in interest in my career and what I wanted to do with theatre. We had conversations about work, shows, future plans, future dreams, and what we thought was good and conversely, what we thought was bad. There was never an academic lens on these conversations—it was more focused on the real world aspects of being a theatre-artist.

That's how it's always been with Robert Richmond. We talk. And through that, I've been defibrillated where I stand sometimes—shocked back into existence with a new point-of-view.

As tech-week for *As You Like It* approached, I became anxious to see what the final product would be. Our rehearsals had utilized a lot of movement and tempo altering, so I knew we were going into tech-week with a show that was uniquely staged. I had every expectation that this show's production values were going to be a little "extra". Not to mention, Richmond had plainly said many times that one of his goals was "to do for Shakespeare what Cirque Du Soleil had done for the Circus". He sought to make Shakespeare approachable, desired, and relevant for modern audiences.

I arrived for the first technical rehearsal of *As You Like It* and my expectations were exceeded. Every possible detail had received attention, and the world of the show was still transporting. Seeing the way Drayton Hall came to life through technical attention unlocked another idea that I've adopted as philosophy in my career: "You're only limited by your imagination and your means". Robert never said this, but I feel like I learned it from watching him. His process is one that is filled with taking chances and exploring every possible avenue to tell the story – whether that is focused on character, movement, or ensemble depends on what's lacking at that time.

With this tech rehearsal, I had realized that a director has the ability to create an exciting world for the characters to live in. By working with actors and designers to explore their imagination, uniqueness, and risk-taking—you can truly create a world in which the actors can immerse themselves and that the audience will want to lean in and engage with. The product is the desired effect of collaboration, making everyone a part of the storytelling that's seen onstage.

Now I will stop here to say, that yes—sometimes this sort of creative storytelling can be called *spectacle*. Both Richmond and I have been accused of perpetrating said taboo. But it's all a matter of taste, and as for me: I appreciate it *so much* when it's effectively done. Richmond is one of the few directors I've seen successfully achieve this time after time.

Richmond's attention to detail and his use of creative storytelling is part of his mission as a director: to reward audiences for attending a theatrical production. I'm happy to say that I have adopted that idea whenever I approach a production, as well.

Consider how easy it is to turn on a television, download or stream a movie, or scroll through YouTube or Facebook all damn day. Entertainment is now easy to attain and more importantly, inexpensive. So, if you're willing to pay almost thirty dollars or more for a theatre ticket—shouldn't the production reward you for that? Shouldn't it be engaging? Shouldn't it *do* what the other entertainments usually *won't*: incite creativity inside *you*, the audience member?

It is a noble effort on behalf of a director to reward the audience. I have seen all but one of Richmond's shows here in Columbia, and I've always felt there was something that got my mind rolling and immersed me in the production—I felt rewarded. I can't tell you how many times I've seen shows where it seemed the creative team was being selfish—ultimately creating art for themselves and not for they're paying public.? However, Richmond's shows make me feel transported and engaged – and for that I'm always thankful as an audience member. I try to create a similar experience for those who come to my shows.

I graduated from The University of South Carolina and began working instantly at Trustus Theatre. During the summer between *As You Like It* and directing *Dog Sees God: Confessions of a Teenage Blockhead* at Trustus Theatre, Richmond became an Associate Professor at the University. My collegiate mentor Karla Koskinen took a job in Alabama, so I was thankful there would still be someone in town who I could turn to when I needed some guidance.

The academic school year started up as always, and my rehearsals for *Dog Sees God* were quickly approaching opening. I invited Richmond to a rehearsal in hopes that he would offer some criticism, and he attended and did just that. However, during the rehearsal he had just witnessed a bit where one of the characters slowly exited a post-funeral scene holding two folding chairs. Richmond stood up and asked me where the aforementioned chairs were kept, and I gave him their location. He walked away from me, and the next thing I saw was Richmond in the bar at Trustus moving through the space using the chairs as wings. At some point he felt he had explored enough with the chairs and watched the rest of the rehearsal.

After we were finished rehearsing, Richmond came up to me and offered some thoughts on how to make certain characters' journeys clearer. I finally asked, "Well what about the chairs? What were you doing in there?" He then said he felt like the character could use the chairs as wings when exiting, and it was just a thought and that I could take it or leave it. I tried this out the next night, and felt like a whole new dynamic had been uncovered in that scene.

The result was injecting more storytelling into the transition and creating another opportunity for the audience to incite their own creativity and turn that image into something real for them. It also brought back that element of paying attention to the tiniest details and rewarding the audience.

If the reader is at all familiar with my work in Columbia, you'll understand what an impact this thought process has had on the productions I've directed. When Robert directs, the story never ends. Transitions aren't a time to go to black and change a bed sheet, they're crucial moments leading from the last scene and exploding into the next moment. He knows the audience never wants to be asked to not care or tune out. They want to be taken on this journey with the actors, and Robert Richmond effectively does this in all that he does. He never lets the story let go of your hand as an audience member—he begs you and seduces you into following the story through to its climax.

Richmond is still working at the university, and he's directed a lot of wonderful productions there. He's also been very instrumental in giving undergraduates in that department a lot of room to research, grow, and self-produce. As for me, he has given me tools that have worked wonders. These are tools that create ensemble, create vulnerability, makes a production seductive, and begs an audience to attend and to be taken on a journey—and please keep all hands and feet inside the car while the ride is in motion.

Robert Richmond summarizes his mission and

philosophy on his website as thus: "[Robert's] mission is to reinvigorate theatre with imagination, innovation and relevance. His directing philosophy is to inspire artists to respond not only intellectually but also, and perhaps more importantly, instinctually—to explore space, time, physicality, and relationships in unique and creative ways." Basically, Richmond says in two sentences what took me pages to say. I'm lucky to live in a town that supports me and the work I do. I'm lucky that Robert Richmond was one of those instrumental people who instilled a theatrical approach in me, and that he lives right here in this city. I owe a lot of my bravery and success to his tutelage—he's made me into a risk taker and he's led me to trust myself. He's showed me the way to impart the same to my casts. I constantly look forward to the next pint or cup of coffee with him, because without fail—I will be inspired again. That's the mark of a great mentor—which he is. And for that—I'm blessed and thankful.

Terrance Hayes

Punches in the Dark

This ink. This name. This Blood. This Blunder.

By Ray McManus

When you're a boy growing up in rural South Carolina, and you want to be a poet, you should first learn to fight. Watch Saturday morning cartoons. Go to church. Get high. And above all, learn how things work by breaking them. There is nothing else to do. The white kids hang out behind gas stations and in pipelines. The black kids play basketball. Sometimes they get together. Some have their own agenda, but for the most part, whether we were stoned or anxious, we fought. From the outside, some would call it boxing, some wrestling, or *wrasseling,* where the side of a pickup truck was as good as any rope, the right height for launching into a flying clothesline from the turnbuckle. But we called it growing up. We learned to jab; we learned takedowns. There were rules. You learned to size up; you learned to keep your mouth shut. On the court or in a field, it didn't matter; I had a hard time doing either. More often than not, I didn't throw the first punch.

I probably knew Terrance Hayes well before I ever read a poem of his or saw him on stage. We grew up basically down the road from each other. Born less than a year apart, he and I would have at least touched circles. He grew up in Columbia, I grew up ten miles away in Lexington—surely there was a game, a party, a bar in the mid-nineties where we caught the same whiff of muscle and smoky perfume. But even if I did know Terrance, I wouldn't have known he was a poet no more than I knew I was a poet. Like me, he kept a secret. Like me, he was on a different path. Like me, he found poetry by accident.

He's a pretty kid, too. I don't know, I got a problem if I should fuck him or fight him.

I'll admit I wasn't sure what to make of Terrance Hayes when I first met him. I was still fighting—going bare-knuckled, toe-to-toe with the past and present. I had just finished my MFA and was sticking around Columbia for my Ph.D. He was publishing *Muscular Music* in a steel town. I had heard he was a good looking man. I don't know why I always heard that. I was trying to write and be my own poet. I wasn't interested in reading brand new poets just yet. I wasn't sure what my reactions would be, if it was going to be a love affair or a fight. As extreme as that sounds, those were the only choices I gave myself. I didn't know any better.

So Kwame Dawes hands me some books to read and a poster to hang in the hallway for Terrance's upcoming reading. His picture on the poster was no joke. This was by far the most handsome poet I had ever seen. Granted the halls are not loaded with the good looking poets, and I know because they are my brothers, but damn he is good looking man. Not pretty like I imagined, but strong, inviting. And there were two books, one for each hand. Two fists like thunder cracking open as their spines hit the desktop. Everything I wanted to be, but couldn't; everything I could've done, but didn't. Poem after poem, punching gristle and sex, with a voice that was brave and disarming—I believed them because I knew them, and I was angry that I didn't write them. I know most people won't understand it when I say I generally respect poets who I am pretty sure would kick my ass. Terrance has incredible reach, and he is the epitome of smooth. He would be a nightmare to contend with in the ring.

And who I am to talk? He's well on his way to being champion of the world. I am barely a contender. But studying his moves, his verbal assault cast in a hazy voice, he is like locking up with the skill of Muhammad Ali and the glib of Apollo Creed. Every jab is careful, delicate, and deliberate. There is a boast in his voice, a survivor's boast, a-been-there-and-done-that-bitches-ain't-shit voice. His poems read like a punch to the face, and instead of crying you just stand there shocked by the sheer brilliance of it. Tender and tight, every poem holding musicality I only wish I could possess. And it didn't matter how personal it was. It didn't matter how removed I was culturally from what the poet was sharing, I got it. It made sense. Each poem telling me something I should have already known, teaching me something I thought I already knew. I wanted to kick his ass. I was convinced it was the only way I could ever be better than him. Then I saw him.

I knew nothing.

Superman don't need no seat belt.

It wasn't the best poem in *Hip Logic*, but it was the most brilliant thing I had ever seen. So simple. So tough. One line, "We sliced the watermelon into smiles," repeated 14 times with the title "Sonnet." It takes balls to pull off something like that. In high school, we measured our balls in the locker room by seeing who could do the most pull ups and hold their breath after without passing out. Sometimes we would pass around a brown bottle to huff. We called it *Rush.* If you didn't do it, you were a narc and suddenly you would have no place to go on a weekend night. One time we were playing soccer, and the coach came up to me and told me I was one of the best ball handlers he had seen in a long time. He also told me that I should get a haircut. I never played soccer again. That was how I grew up. If I liked it, I did well, if I didn't then I didn't. Call it therapy. Call it the willingness to forgo and forget. Call it chicken shit. I'll never have balls like Terrance Hayes.

Even the dirt dreams of it now.

It is two roads along two rivers,

The sky above a mother's face

The day her husband leaves

For war. No blood and stars

But the blood and stars.

Let's find it and break its fucking neck,

Let's break its fucking jaw.

—from *Wind in a Box*

Terrance's poems glide smooth and tight, like the sprinter's muscle stretched just before s/he takes the block. That isn't alarming since other poets possess and have possessed the same ability for thousands of years. But what separates a poem by Terrance from many poets, and certainly a lot of contemporary poets, is that he is simply unafraid to fly. I am too cautious at times. Perhaps I am making up for the times when I wasn't cautious. But I know I install safety nets around every poem I write, and I have to work very hard to convince myself that what I am writing is important or that anyone cares. You don't get that feeling reading a poem by Terrance Hayes. There is a purpose, and urgency that you just don't find often. It's not cockiness. It's not aggression. It's confidence—the same kind of confidence you would have concerning gravity or in your ability to blink. Taking flight with Terrance is never reckless. You know he knows where he's going. You trust it. Why hold back?

*I would eat you, were it not for the pain
of my big tooth wiggling like one of those small doors
cut into doors so that pets, small dogs mostly,
can come and go as they please. What I have eaten of you
tastes like mint and damp clay, tastes exactly like the soil
I ate in my grandmother's yard as a boy. They called
me savage then, because I reeked and wreaked havoc
on the slim flowers so well acquainted with the sun.*

   —from Whatever Happened to the Fine
   Young Cannibals

Yeah, Boy. I'm too cool. Don't talk to me.

Both times I met Terrance, I hardly said a word. Not out of anger or a want to be silent then deadly. Rather I was star struck. I've never been cool, really. I just did things. People said they were cool, so I kept doing those things. And when I did something that warranted the "not cool" reprimand I stopped. The man is cool. His walk, his talk, everything about him is cool, and you get the impression that Terrance never did anything uncool. His poems are not full of militant black fists. They are not oozing sex through some tough boy bravado. There is pain in there. There is longing. There is tenderness. Terrance is unashamed to let us inside the speaker. It is an empowering act and one that requires the utmost humility. We see the failure and success and celebrate them equally. We see the hope and the despair and find ourselves laughing and crying at the same time. A part of us would expect no less, but how often are we let down by the poet's inability to accept the fact that they are only one word away from complete failure. How often have we been eluded by a poet who is basically full of shit, that we are led to believe some greatness exists because someone told us so. Everybody likes the cool kid. Think *Happy Days*. No one went around pretending to be Richie Cunningham. Everyone wanted to be the Fonz. But the Fonz, for all his leather and denim, was fake. He wasn't cool. He was just different. With one or two exceptions (the jukebox fist bump and learning to read), he never really did anything cool. It was too easy to just say *HEEEY*. There is no risk in that. It takes a lot of risk to just be a little cool. If Terrance wasn't willing to take the risk in his poems, I am not so sure we would be as eager to read them.

I loved Bruce Lee and a ten dollar ukulele.

For my little mutt Shepherd and the saplings,

I performed black Superman melodramas barefoot

On the picnic table until a toenail opened

On my big toe like the hood of the father's Lincoln

And a fever broke. I dropped stuff.

I showed Erica (my queen) McQueen

My junior penis. I showed Connie Simpson,

The Limelight

I showed Meko Jackson, I showed Precious Jones,

And again and again they split like pigtails

On a trampoline...

—from *The Blue Terrance*

It's just a job. Grass grows, birds fly, waves pound the sand. I beat people up.

If I had to do it all over again, I would've never thrown my knee into Carol Corley's face. I would've paid more attention to the street signs on paved roads. I would've listened more. I would've gone somewhere. I would've saved my knuckles. Terrance Hayes is everything I am not as a poet—a Whiting Award winner, a National Book award winner, tall. But I think there are more similarities between us than differences. I think he and I are really brothers separated at birth and I got bleached. I don't want to fight him or fuck him. I don't want to be him. I need him. I need him to beat me up. I need him to keep writing the poems I should've written. I need him to keep being all the things that I can't. So I can.

Notes

"This ink. This name. This Blood. This Blunder" is from the poem "Wind in a Box" from the book by the same title by Terrance Hayes.

"He's a pretty kid, too. I don't know, I got a problem if I should fuck him or fight him" is from *Raging Bull* starring Robert De Niro. Jake is talking to Como about the fight he has coming up with Janiro.

"Superman don't need no seat belt" is from *Muhammad Ali*.

"Yeah, Boy. I'm too cool. Don't talk to me" is from the poem "Blue Kool" from the *Wind in a Box* by Terrance Hayes.

"It's just a job. Grass grows, birds fly, waves pound the sand. I beat people up" is from *Muhammad Ali*.

Stacey Calvert

Reluctant Teacher

By Bonnie Boiter-Jolley

When I first met Stacey Calvert over a decade ago, she explained to me how being a dancer is a very selfish thing. As a dancer it is always about *you*. *You* must think about *your* health, *your* rest, *your* energy, *your* nutrition, *your* body, *your* conditioning, *your* rehearsal, *your* preparedness, *your* performance, and *your* choices when on stage. Had I known better at the time I might have told her that for teachers and coaches, especially teachers and coaches like Stacey, it is really quite the opposite. Teachers, at least the good ones, are generous. They are giving of their time, knowledge, experiences, patience, advice, guidance, and understanding. Stacey is just that. Not only generous, but gracious. It is often that she has listened to my complaints and offered any number of the above gifts. Not only has she taught me new and better ways of dancing and, for that matter, thinking about dance, but she has shared with me her contagious passion, however reluctant at first, for teaching.

The daughter of Naomi Calvert—one half of the founding mothers of Columbia's legendary Calvert-Brody School of Dance—Stacey was born into the world of dance and grew up surrounded by the school her mother had built and loved. But for me as a professional dancer, and for a great many other perpetual students of dance,

Stacey Calvert is the one who has rebuilt, remodeled, and renovated Columbia's house of higher dance education since returning to her home after a career dancing in two of the best ballet companies in the world. When I first enrolled at the University of South Carolina and joined the dance program in its early years of being more than just a mediocre college program, I became part of a small group of highly dedicated, professional caliber dancers who were drawn to the program primarily to work with and, if we were lucky, be molded by Stacey. A fairly new faculty member at the time, Stacey still had trouble accepting herself as a teacher. But in the four years I studied under her, I danced some of the most challenging roles, and learned some of the most difficult, yet valuable, lessons of my life.

To be a young dancer from South Carolina, I have been fortunate to have had a number of great mentors in the more than two dozen years that I've studied dance—the late great American ballerinas Melissa Hayden and Rebecca Wright, for example, as well as Anna Marie Holmes, and the Bolshoi's Shamil Yagudin—but no one else can compare when it comes to the impact Stacey has had on my life both as a professional dancer, and as the reluctant teacher I have become myself. Stacey teaches ballet in a manner that makes her students not only believe, but trust her. With an electricity that seems to radiate from her with sizzle and zaps, she explains the anatomy, physicality, common sense, and science of dancing. There is no doubting her devotion to the art of dance.

Stacey is the first teacher I encountered who uses her own experiences, and often difficult lessons learned, to teach her students relatable concepts. As a veteran dancer with the New York City Ballet who bore the standard of the great choreographer and Father of American Ballet George Balanchine, by learning from the man himself, she has plenty of experience from which to draw.

At 17, Calvert moved to New York City to study at the prestigious School of American Ballet. In her second year at the school, she was asked by the Artistic Director and founder of the New York City Ballet, George Balanchine to join the company. Shortly after, however, the legendary choreographer passed away leaving Calvert to wait another season to be invited once more by his successor, Peter Martins. Nine years of *corps de ballet* work later, Calvert made a risky move, taking a leave from the company to travel to Frankfurt, Germany to work with innovative choreographer William Forsythe. When Calvert returned to NYCB the next season after sustaining a broken arm, she was greeted with roles in five new Diamond Project works and a promotion to soloist rank.

Calvert doesn't teach solely from her impressive past though. On the contrary, she is constantly exploring technique, researching and gathering data on the movement of the human instrument, and in turn revising and amending her theories. I remember a specific instance in class when Stacey stopped in the middle of giving an exercise, and as the light bulb went on in her head, explained that she had at that moment realized why frappe is executed in a visible fifth position. As it turns out, and she will reiterate time and again, everything in ballet somewhat confusingly takes place in this most crossed and rotated position. Somehow when Stacey explains it, it makes sense. It is this perpetual study of the art form that connects Calvert with her students. On many occasions she has commented that she wished she had known when she was dancing what she has learned from being a teacher. Calvert's authentic and honest efforts at problem solving offer her students the opportunity to learn along with her.

Five years after Calvert's return to NYCB, she gave birth to daughter, Ayla, with then husband and fellow dancer and choreographer Kevin O'Day. As marital bliss faded, Stacey returned to South Carolina to raise her daughter as a single mother. The energizer bunny embodied, she seems never to run out of gas. Petite and wiry without an ounce of fat on her body, she wears her blonde hair cropped closed to her head, perfectly framing her intense blue eyes. She bounds between Charleston and Columbia, from yoga to Gyrotonic classes, the University of South Carolina Dance facility to the Columbia Music Festival Association with stops at Heathwood Hall for daughter Ayla and Starbucks coffee somewhere in between. Strongly opinionated and relentless in her ideals, she faces every daily challenge with vigor and intensity.

On an autumn Thursday afternoon after work and before an evening commitment, I meet with Stacey, who is between teaching at the USC Conservatory and the Center for Dance Education across town at the CMFA. We are in a sun-drenched studio for a quick hour of rehearsal. On the menu is a variation from the Balanchine ballet *La Source* (1968) to be performed a few weeks later at the Koger Center. I am honored to be asked to dance as a guest artist for USC, but even more excited to be able to work one-on-one with Stacey like we did in the old days when I was her student. In our 45 minutes together she coaches, advises, gives options, suggestions and ideas. She at once makes my body race and sets my mind at ease. I leave feeling as though a new world has been opened to me and all I must do now is explore it. Stacey has the ability to present dance as a puzzle, a problem with many solutions and a map constantly unfolding on itself. There are endless sets of possibilities, turns one might take, and destinations one might find. As the coach, Stacey is my guide, and she teaches me the consequences of my movement.

As one of Calvert's first students in Columbia, I can vouch that she never planned on wearing the hat of a teacher. But Stacey gives every ounce of energy to her classes and students. I have consciously tried to adopt her energetic and inspiring teaching methods in my own classes. She doesn't believe in teaching from a chair, so I don't either. I recall signature combinations and emphasis on musicality, and try to instill the drive to move in my students. "Be on top of the note," and "don't get light" I quip in recollection of Stacey's words that will stay forever in my mind.

In various photographs of Stacey taken mid-performance, the indication of movement is clear. The sensation that she might, at any moment and with primed muscles, explode from the frozen frame is palpable and I try to explain this to my students as I point to photos on the wall where I teach. Everything, every moment, all the time, is alive and electric. I have a long way to go before I reach Stacey's teaching standards, but for now I have her words running through my mind as I dance and teach.

Every show I have performed with Stacey's coaching has been an experience and a gift. She taught me that our bodies learn the most when they are tired, and perform the best when our brains think we are exhausted. She preaches that there is nothing stagnant about ballet and every movement, large or small, comes from the smallest tendue. She counts only some of the music and sings the rest but knows every note of it and expects every step to arrive on the note. "Show the music," she says.

Perhaps the most remarkable fact about Stacey Calvert, however, is that she is the only person I have ever known to start every class, no matter the day, the challenges or stresses, with a cleansing breath and a smile. Stacey has taught me just how amazing it is that we get to dance.

Vicky Saye Henderson
Leading Lady

By Robbie Robertson

I'll admit it. I was a theatre snob. When it came to local stage productions, it took a great deal to impress me mainly because I sought perfection in others as I aimed for excellence in my own creative pursuits. That said, I was well aware of the differences between community theatre hobbyists who sought a part time creative outlet in their lives and those who were serious about their art. I always had a distinct and unwavering line drawn in the theatrical sandbox between "the professional" and "the amateur" and could easily assess who was who on the local theatre scene.

And quite frankly, just being "local" was an indicator to me that one was really not serious or professional about their craft.

All that changed when I met Vicky Saye Henderson.

I was vaguely aware of Vicky's reputation as Columbia theatre's leading lady du jour and had heard rave reviews about her work. But I had lived in and out of Columbia several times in the past two decades and had seen many Vickys come and go. The better ones had always moved on to NYC and L.A., two cities I had also lived in as I pursued my own passion for theatre and screenwriting.

After finishing the screenwriting program at UCLA, I came back south again for what I imagined as a temporary sabbatical. And even though I was returning to Columbia, I was no less serious about my craft and felt my ongoing west coast connections made me a professional who simply chose to temporarily live elsewhere. Admittedly, I felt like the sole exception to my own judgmental stance on where one has to live to properly pursue their passion–and that's when I finally had a personal introduction to the woman who made me rethink and redefine my ideas of "community" and "theatre."

It was the 2007 Trustus holiday party when we first met. Vicky immediately reminded me of a classic Hitchcock heroine--the cool, old school blonde that listened a lot more than she talked. Vicky had style, grace, and confidence—not to mention a 1000-watt smile that could light up any stage. As we talked, I remembered I had seen her as Janet in a production of *Rocky Horror Picture Show* a memory reignited by her huge smile that could light up any room she entered. During our brief party conversation, Vicky pointedly referred to herself as a "working actor" and a "teaching artist," two terms that caused my inner theatre snob to come out and play. I felt a condescending grin creep across my face as I listened to Vicky describe her "professional" work in Columbia. She talked about her craft, how she chose roles, the numerous classes she taught. Nodding along, I thought to myself that this woman was most likely a "wannabe" who was trapped in an inferior market because of personal responsibilities or perhaps a sense of insecurity.

Whatever the reason, I thought it was a shame that a woman so lovely, so gifted, and so charming was stuck in a place not exactly known for legit theatre.

It wasn't until several years later that Vicky would once again enter my universe. I had begun work on a documentary series pilot I had pitched to a major west coast television production company. (Documentary series is a less offensive code word for "Reality TV," but my idea felt a bit loftier since I would be profiling aspects of southern culture.) I was shooting footage with Larry Hembree, the incoming managing director of Trustus Theatre, when I asked him to identify other major arts players that may prove to be camera worthy. I was attempting to cast the "role" of a local leading lady when Larry suggested Vicky. I immediately remembered that 1000-watt smile and bet it would be equally appealing on camera as on stage.

Since our first encounter at the holiday party several years earlier, Vicky's reputation has only grown around town. I had I recently seen her as the white trash diva of *The Great American Trailer Park Musical,* a role where she dominated the stage with wit, bravura, and a down home invitation to kick up your heels and have a damn good time.

Vicky had become even lovelier and confidant since our first encounter and I eagerly sat her down for a long on camera interview.

Just as she had intrigued me on stage and years before at the party, Vicky revealed more insights into her acting "career," again opening up about her life, her commitment to her craft and her ambition. Vicky reiterated that she thought of herself as a "teaching artist" and that acting and vocal instruction were a very important part of her life. Her eyes lit up when talking about her classes and the impact she could have on others who wished to follow their dreams. She talked about her very first role as a "sexy nurse" in a school production of "The King Who Loved Lollipops" and she laughed that her early typecasting carried on to today. She spontaneously burst into song at several points and she talked about how the various roles she had played helped her with difficult moments in her personal life.

"No matter what I am going through at any point in my own life—whether that's a divorce or raising a child as a single parent, I am able to find direct parallels between my characters' lives and my own," said Vicky. "I'm then able to take the lessons I learn from these women and apply it to my own life."

At this point in the interview, I was deeply touched by her intuitive nature, a firm respect of her craft and a beautifully expressive face that was so damn authentic.

Then she absolutely floored me when she talked about writing goodbye notes to every character she has played, thanking each for the impact they had on her life. With her confidence and unbridled passion so very apparent I was, once again, totally baffled by this woman.

"Why in the hell aren't you taking this big talent to a bigger market," I said aloud. "If you're so touchy feely with these characters and the lessons you are learning, and you sing like a powerhouse and look like you do, then why, Miss Vicky Saye Henderson, why aren't you a big, big star on Broadway or at least doing touring productions of Broadway shows?"

Did she simply suffer from a lack of ambition? Surely someone with that much talent would want to reach her full potential and take it to the next level? Or was it something else? Was it a fear? Was it insecurity?

No, it was something much simpler. Something deeper. Something sweeter. Something much more intimate.

When pressed on her seeming lack of ambition, Vicky Saye Henderson admitted that she simply sought something all of us try to achieve in life—balance.

"Years ago, I made the choice to live in Columbia because it gave me the balanced life I need," Vicky said. "I have friends here. I helped raise a son here. This is home to me and I'm connected here."

"I get the opportunity to do things that other actors in other markets only dream of," she said.

Vicky reiterated that she was not driven by fame or fortune but nonetheless did not consider herself any less ambitious than other actors in larger markets.

Vicky Saye Henderson was simply content to bloom where she was planted—in a place that she loved to call home.

And that's when Vicky Saye Henderson, the teaching artist, taught me a very valuable lesson—that art and creative expression should never be quantified. Theatre and any type of personal expression should never be judged or labeled as amateur or professional. There is merit in every experience and at every realm of existence. I could still pursue screenwriting and TV projects with my "big Hollywood connections" but like Vicky, I could also get great satisfaction by being near friends and family and embracing the South—a place that inspires my work time and time again. Vicky also reminded me of the intrinsic value of community theatre and how it should be a revered place where people of all levels come together to share their love of the arts.

Most important, Vicky, the actor and teaching artist, reminded me that a professional isn't always the one who's most famous or making the most money. Sometimes the professional is the one who is the most passionate and that's something that can never be defined by place.

And when asked if she would ever abandon her beloved city for a bigger market, Vicky Saye Henderson says that Columbia provides her with real life connective experiences that make her a better artist and she is more than happy to return the favor for the place she calls home.

"I am so lucky to be on the front line of making Columbia a better place to live," Vicky said. "I'm just a small part of a cultural renaissance that is enhancing the quality of life for others. And for any actor—no matter where you are—that's the role of a lifetime."

Robert Lamb

Courage

By James D. McCallister

Fear.

Like most people who survive into their late 20s and beyond, by that age I'd experienced the emotion in any number of terrible forms, but nothing like what I was about to endure, a new kind of terror like out of a bad dream: the idea of exposing myself before a room full of strangers.

No, not like when one dreams about showing up late for class wearing only skivvies—or worse, the birthday suit—but close enough: I had to face a classroom of fellow aspiring writers, all of whom I suspected of being far beyond my abilities, and none more than the instructor: a mature, gentle Southern novelist and former Georgia newspaperman named Robert Lamb. The class was called Fiction Workshop. He'd told us to call him Bob, and taught us that literature wasn't a static object frozen in amber to be studied; it was an art form that lived and breathed in all of us.

I'd wait outside the building after class to catch the genial professor of literature, bending his ear and talking up my ambition to write, and to be published, and what it all meant. About the books and authors that meant something to me. I was hungry to interact with someone who'd made it—who'd seen his name in print, which hadn't occurred since the high school newspaper, and on one short story published in a one-shot literary magazine produced on a mimeograph machine in the school secretary's office, and all of that now ten years in the past.

"It's a red letter day when you finally get published," he said, standing in the fading Carolina autumn light, leaves blowing across the paved walkway between the classroom buildings.

"You must feel really accomplished when it happens," I said.

"Feels pretty good."

———

Now, though, it was halfway through the semester, and I had to do more than make small talk, more than cut bait—I had to fish.

I had to read.

I stood aquiver behind the lectern in the University of South Carolina classroom, one of those terraced auditoriums of long tables and fixed, swiveling plastic chairs that can hold a few dozen students comfortably. The room wasn't full, not by a long shot, but full enough. Thought I'd hurl; as if I hadn't been anxious enough, I'd had about a quart of coffee, and stomach acid gurgled and roiled in the depths of my body.

Was there depth in my writing, though? I hadn't a clue.

Sure, in undergrad I'd stood before judges and peers to 'perform' scripts I'd written, had taken speech and acting classes, had made a film and suffered through its first (and only) public viewing, but I'd never read fiction aloud. Hell—I'd barely let anyone, my wife included, so much as peek at the work. But here I'd been cajoled by this real writer to reveal myself before him. Before them all.

The guy that'd read the week before, a lawyer in his 40s, had produced engaging and mature-sounding work that read funny and polished to a spit-shine. He'd set the bar, and set it high—his sounded like a mature voice. He did have twenty years on me, but at the moment, all I knew was that he sounded like a real writer, in control of his craft and voice.

Speaking of voices, that afternoon I'd sat at my desk at work, but instead of cataloguing archival newsreel footage backed up on a stack of VHS cassettes, I read one last time through the chapter I'd chosen. As I whispered aloud and compared the work to that of the lawyer, I thought mine sounded clunky and overwritten. Trying too hard. Grim, unfunny, a slog—an inveterate drunk buries his beloved pet dog. Sheesh.

But it was too late. I had to read. Bob Lamb was expecting, if not greatness, then at least courage.

That night as I began to read, my voice echoed strange and strained in the room of expectant faces, Bob's most of all—I'd talked up my chops. I avoided their eyes, his especially.

I don't remember every second of that reading, but I do recall taking careful note of which words and sentences sounded right, which ones didn't, and how I tried hard to invest my narrative with vocal gravitas. The class received this work in silence; afterwards I was told by both students and the instructor that, whatever flaws my work possessed, I'd nonetheless acquitted myself well.

As had become the norm, outside the Humanities building I hung around and made small talk with Bob. I told him I felt lighter of spirit. That I'd passed a certain test—I'd read my work before peers, but hadn't burst into flames or collapsed and died under the glare of their judgment.

"You should be proud—the pages you read in there tonight were as good as any I've heard from the MFA students," the professor of literature told me.

"Do you really think that?"

His shrug, slight, nonetheless spoke volumes. "Wouldn't say it if I didn't mean it."

I could have floated all the way home.

But for all sorts of reasons, many I still don't fully understand, I didn't keep writing, not through the fruition of that novel, or any other, not for a long time—I hadn't yet found the thread. Despite Bob's praise, I didn't believe in myself, or the work. Not yet.

———

Ten years later my life had changed radically, but I hadn't become a novelist—I'd left the film archive to become, alongside my wife, a retail business owner. A learning curve, one vastly different from either archiving media, or writing stories and novels. In other words, a path I hadn't anticipated.

But a good one, an iconoclastic voyage that felt a closer fit with what I'd come to realize were my true goals: rather than as a cog in a machine, I sought an independent, bohemian lifestyle—that's what I'd wanted out of the writing, wasn't it? The artist's life, the creative grind, a different sort of workaday experiential existence?

And as for the creativity my prior career had lacked, try keeping a customer base satisfied, as well as representing the face of hippie subculture here in Columbia, in an era when the years since Jerry Garcia's passing quickly began to add up.

The proof was in the profit, however, and the business, by any measure, was a success. I'd merely bought into a successful retail shop, however—I still had much to prove to myself about what and where I was supposed to be in life, and what I could achieve. I had stories to tell.

―

Big news: a new grocery store, a Publix, had opened in Columbia's downtown Vista district—not all that exciting, no, but it'd be on the way home from Five Points, where our store was, and is, located. The convenience of an upscale grocer into which to duck on the drive home, or on the way in to grab-and-go a tray of sushi for lunch, meant I could save a few minutes out of an average day, which I desperately needed—three years into my new life as a businessman, at the turn of the millennium I'd decided to begin writing again: a dream deferred, but never forgotten.

Since that moment a few years had passed, and I could report that I was no longer a complete neophyte—a short story had won a prize from a respected west coast literary journal, one that'd published writers like Bukowski. Not only that, but I'd finally finished that long-gestating novel, and was well into my second. Despite my progress, I didn't feel that I was quite 'there,' but well on my way.

Not long after my short story triumph, I'm made one of those visits to the new downtown grocer, and who did I find standing in that shiny, bustling new store but my first, and in a way the only true writing mentor I'd ever had: Bob Lamb. He stood by a stack of books—a gritty urban mystery called Atlanta Blues that had come out to good notices—watching shoppers push by with their cartloads of sustenance, seemingly oblivious to the presence in their midst of an accomplished author.

I found the encounter serendipitous, and told him so—I'd at long last finished a draft of the novel I'd begun over a decade before, a sprawling, Conroyesque Southern family epic that had come in at an unwieldy and bloated 1200-page monster of a sloppy first draft.

"You should come talk to my class about your writing," he said. He explained that he loved having other writers as guest speakers, and as a former student, my recent success, he joked, was testimony to his teaching methods. "They'd love to hear about it. And so would I."

I flashed back to my first reading—I had a pang of an old familiar terror. "Well—sure," I said, feigning courage. "Anytime."

"How about next week?"

I gulped, said I'd be there.

So, I read, and discussed the work. In my Bob Lamb class, an evening session, there'd been mainly adult continuing education students, but here I saw young, fresh faces. I read my pages thinking that much time had passed since I was the age of these folks.

The students, and Bob, were receptive to my reading, and the story behind the composition of the long and difficult literary novel I'd produced. One young woman seemed mildly aghast, however, that I'd first tried to write a version of the book so long ago, that its ultimate completion would have bridged the Bush, Clinton, and Bush regimes.

Not Bob—he understood. "These novels," he said with a familiar shrug, "sometimes take many years to get done right. Or never at all."

I'd guest lecture in Bob Lamb's fiction workshop on a number of other occasions, each time with good results—perhaps especially when the work didn't go over like I'd hoped, which allowed me to discuss it with a room full of instant critics, and learn from my mistakes. I was thickening the skin in a manner necessary to any writer worth his ambition. For this, too, I now had Bob to thank.

———

Two years later, and I'm downtown in Columbia's lovely convention center, a place that, for this weekend, anyway, is one of books, and authors, and readers.

I'd come to the South Carolina Book Festival to take what they billed as a master class; in this case one in which an editor and an agent would inform a ballroom of would-be scribes what it took to get published in today's marketplace, yadda-yadda, an idea that was never more on my mind than that dreary February afternoon: Now I had three completed manuscripts sitting on the hard drive or in various drafts I'd printed, oftentimes, I thought, merely to remind myself that the work was real, that the pages were accumulating.

Maybe it's time for an agent, I thought. Maybe I can pitch the one teaching the class; maybe he or she will see the potential and ask for pages. Stranger things, I thought, have surely happened.

But before the class even starts, who do I find in a seat but Bob Lamb, author of the Pen-Hemingway nominee *Striking Out*, a book that'd informed my latest novel, and the thriller *Atlanta Blues*.

Bob, not on the dais, but in the audience. "Why on earth are you taking this class?" I asked. "You're published!"

He offered me that modest Lamb shrug I'd come to know: "There's always more to learn."

By now, with three novels under my belt—my long-gestating literary effort, another ambitious piece that sought to make sense of my Grateful Dead experience, and that latest effort, a coming-of-age saga that in length and scope seemed smaller than my others, so small that I could barely see its 200 pages peeking up over the stacks of drafts of the first two manuscripts—

I'd come to believe that I was ready for the next step, which was trying concrete steps toward getting one of them in print.

By the end of the session, however, I didn't feel very optimistic about my chances of getting an agent, much less getting published—my material wasn't high concept enough. Didn't fit into genres, except maybe the coming-of-age saga about loss of innocence, the small fry of my three children. That one, easy enough to describe: a kind of literary American Graffiti, one set in late '70s Myrtle Beach. Drugs. Sex. Intrigue and danger. I never even got a chance to pitch it, but I did get the agent's card.

Bob, too, seemed disheartened—he might have already been published, and taught a university-level class about writing fiction, but he still harbored ambition to break through on another level. I understood completely—I wanted that kind of validation as well. What artist worth his efforts doesn't aim high?

At one time, Bob had had a big-time agent, Julian Bach, who'd also represented Pat Conroy. But that'd been a long time ago, he said, and hadn't resulted in much action. "Some writers I know say they wouldn't have an agent if you paid them to."

Frustration bubbled over in the lobby—"I'm ready," I blurted, not really believing it. Mainly because I wasn't ready, not in the way I thought, but considering about all the work I'd put in, especially on the latest project, which thanks to both its setting and theme I called *King's High-*

way, a yawning need burned inside to prove to myself that I had written a book good enough to be accepted, published, and read. The rejection slips I'd acquired on my first two books hadn't been encouraging ones, either—they'd simply been cold rejections, a growing pile, and deep down I knew both manuscripts needed work, perhaps years more. *King's Highway,* not so much. It felt complete and whole, only rough around the edges.

"I just need someone to take a chance on me," I continued to Bob. "On this new novel I've written."

Bob asked me to tell him about it, and on the walk into the exhibit hall, I did.

On the front row of vendors, he led me over to a table—Red Letter Press, an imprint that'd been started here in Columbia by none other than Bob himself. He told me about his plans, how he wanted to make it possible for writers to get published. To enjoy that Red Letter day. It was getting too hard to break through to 'publisher's row,' as the big houses are known. Writers deserved a chance, echoing my own words.

"So, I'd love to read King's Highway," he said, taking his place behind the table where he had a few titles for sale, including collections of stories written by former students, and a series of children's mystery novels by Karen Petit that were attracting a great deal of attention from buyers. "We're looking for good material to publish."

I went home as fast as the wind would carry

me and printed off a copy, an act as important as any I'd taken in my so-called writing career up to that point: By the end of the summer I'd have my first novel in print, but not until after it'd had some further revision and refinement—working with an editor was nerve-wracking, but useful and edifying.

Especially being that my editor was Bob, who is as genial and kind a collaborator, publisher, and friend as anyone could want. He believed in the work. He believed in me. I may not have been ready, not like I thought, but he could see that I was getting there, and saw value in helping me to achieve my lifelong dream.

What a fine teacher, this—above and beyond the call.

Bob Lamb's not only one of the best and most humane of literary-minded authors, he's also a beloved husband and father, a sage and a saint for wanting to show us a vision of the world through his literary lens. Born just across the river in Augusta, Bob has nonetheless earned his place in the pantheon of South Carolina writers, with the worst news being that Columbia has now lost him to life on the balmy coast, where I hope he will produce many more novels and stories. The honor of knowing him remains mine, but his contributions to the canon of Southern literature, whether already published or soon to be written, belong to all of us.

Greg Leevy

The Youngest and the Sweetest

"...he comes before us still, a towering figure, laughing and weeping, with parables and paradoxes, so generous, so amusing, and so right."

Oscar Wilde

By Alex Smith

Hard to believe, come January, that he'll be gone for four years.

I'm not sure what I was doing at home on the night of January 5. I was still constantly running in those days, especially at night. My friend, who worked with him, called and told me that Bougie had been in the hospital for some time. She explained what he had been diagnosed with, reassured me that his family was with him, and, finally, let me know that he had fallen into a coma that day and was not expected to live through the night. Hearing these words felt like swallowing glass. Every single one was news to me—furious, devastating, and terminal news that, like many others who knew him, I didn't think I would actually live to hear. Bougie was an institution, a monument, a monumental human being. All I could do was catch my breath and whisper, "I didn't even know he was sick." Bougie died early the next morning.

I remembered a conversation I'd had with another mutual friend (it seems like everyone I ever met knew Bougie) back when fall was beginning in 2008. I dropped in on him at his house, and he was pacing, smoking, frantic. When I came inside he hugged me hard and told me that he was very glad I'd come over. He'd just found out earlier that day that, "an old girlfriend" of his was sick. "How sick?" I asked. "Big sick," he responded, "the big sick." He went on, was vague, said he couldn't tell me who she was or whether I knew her, said he knew that "she" was going to beat this thing. He was too frantic, too scattered, to belie how deeply sad he was, or how well I actually knew his "old girlfriend". I didn't know it at the time, but I believe that's when I found out that Bougie was dying.

———

I met Greg Leevy on the first day of rehearsals for the second run of *Angels in America, Part I, Millennium Approaches* by Tony Kushner in 1996. I assistant directed the show for my mentor, the amazing Jayce Tromsness, at Trustus Theatre. The cast member who had played the role of Belize had moved to Asheville, North Carolina between runs, so we had to recast. Everyone insisted that Greg was perfect to play Belize.

We worked like dogs on the original run of *Angels.* It had been a major financial and artistic success (an oddity, then as now). The show was, as has often been said since, the Trustus show. The fact that we got the rights to do this monumental show (which had won the Pulitzer Prize for drama, countless New York awards, and had only, at the point of our production, been produced in major cities around the world), the fact that we managed not only not to fuck it up, but to create a beautiful, original staging which was adored by audiences and critics, and which sold out to standing room only crowds, was a badge of credibility for Trustus and everyone involved with it, from top to bottom.

It was also the mountain's height to which all that followed after it could never quite measure up. I still, almost twenty years later, count it among maybe the ten best shows I've ever worked on. It followed that we were all very protective of the production, especially the younger, and, typically, much more serious of us working on it. The chemistry was so perfect in the first run that, I thought, it seemed like tempting fate to mess with it. I went into the first rehearsal that Bougie would be at up on my hind legs with the fur around my neck standing up. I was ready to tear this new guy apart.

Instead, of course, I was charmed pantsless by the guy. The balls with which he took over the role of Belize made everyone rethink the role completely. I'd seen actors disappear into their roles, but this was the first time I think I'd seen a role disappear into the actor. It was as though the words had just been waiting for him to say them. He was perfect.

When we were introduced, he told me his name, and then said, "...but my friends call me Bougie." I asked him what "Bougie" meant, and I'll never forget what he said or how he said it. He looked at me without a hint of sarcasm, but with what I was to discover was his trademark languor, and said, "The youngest and the sweetest." It wasn't until many years later that I realized that he had been bullshitting, but it didn't matter. From that moment on, he was Bougie to me.

One year, I got the gig to direct a couple of Late Night productions at Trustus, the first of which was to be one of my favorite plays of all time, *The Maids* by Jean Genet. It was a difficult undertaking, as Genet's complete play ran something close to two hours straight through. I was forced to do something I despise, cutting significant portions of the dialogue, in order to make it fit into the one-act/one hour standard held by the Late Night programming at the time. I was surprised, though, that after I'd snipped major bits of Genet's poetry, that I ended up with a tight, mostly cohesive plot which lent itself to the comedy inherent in the story without losing the ultimate poignancy of the maids' liberation. So far so good.

I cast the play according to Genet's stated wishes, with a couple of very attractive men in their early twenties in the roles of Claire and Solange. I played upon the singular mention of two usually unseen characters, "…those idiots the cook and the butler…," and had Claire and Solange revert a step beyond their usual subservience when The Madame showed up, sluffing off even their Maid drag to reveal that they were, in fact, the Cook and the Butler. There was only one real choice to fill the role of The Madame. When I approached Bougie with my plan for telling the story (he was a huge Genet fan, too), he was more than game to shave, shower, don the requisite wig, heels and evening-wear, and become my Madame.

From a plot standpoint, there were very few of The Madame's lines that could be cut. Virtually every moment of her Harry Lime-like appearance in the story serves to either illustrate her relationship with the doomed Claire and Solange, or to justify the horrific caricature they take turns portraying her as.

I can't remember what the circumstances were, but I was talking with then Managing Director Kay Thigpen about the show and how rehearsals were going, the ups and downs of it all. Kay, as long as I've known her, has always been one of the most unflappable people I've ever known. But I had never seen her react in quite so emphatic a way as she did when I casually mentioned the expositional importance of The Madame's character, and that, in order to make sure that the audience was clear that this was more than just a Monty Python sketch, "I told Bougie to really take his time."

I am not being hyperbolic when I say that Kay gasped, and that her eyes widened so suddenly and completely that I thought she might have been having a heart attack. "Do not *ever* tell Bougie to take his time," she warned.

I promised her that I would convey to him that I meant he should take his time, "within reason," but it was too late, and, as I often discovered was the case in the many years I worked at Trustus, Kay was right. *The Maids*, which I was mostly happy with, ran almost ninety-five minutes, making it one of, if not the, longest Late Night show to run at Trustus to that point, a fact which Kay never let me live down, and which she would console me about by patting me on the back and saying, "If only you hadn't told Bougie to take his time…"

—

Bougie could, and would, make fun of you, but (unlike just about everybody else in the theatre) he would do it to your face and in such an honest way that you couldn't help but take it for what it was worth, and love him more for it. I know, because it happened to me when I found myself onstage in a Late Night production Bougie was directing, Douglas Turner Ward's 1965 play *A Day of Absence.* The conceit of this comedy was simple and ingenious: One day, the white residents of an unnamed city in the Jim Crow South awake to find that all of the black residents have mysteriously and completely disappeared. The gist of the story is that these white yokels can barely get along without their black counterparts, and the whole proceeding is made even more hilarious because it is written to be performed (almost) entirely by African-Americans in white-face...a reverse minstrel show!

The one actual white role in the play (which Ward, tongue firmly in cheek, explains in his introductory notes for the play is included in order to, "...subvert any charge that the production is unintegrated.") is an East coast, Dan Rather-like television news announcer who, late in the titular day, swoops down into the town to interview its white inhabitants about the impact of the black citizens' disappearance. About a page and a half of monologue, two pages of dialogue...

I approached Bougie, having read and loved the script, and told him that I wanted to play The Announcer, that I would come in off book, and that I could be there for the first read-through and then for the five nights prior to opening, since I was also in the eight o'clock show. He seemed worried that I might be stretching myself a little thin, but I reminded him that the character

I was playing at eight had a total of about five lines, and that I wouldn't even have to change since the eight o'clock character wore a tweed suit and tie that would look perfect on a 1960s television reporter. Bougie acquiesced, and we were off.

I went to the first reading, then bade farewell for several weeks to go rehearse the eight o'clock show, returning the Sunday night before *A Day of Absence* opened. As promised, I had my lines memorized, and I quickly learned my blocking so that by Tuesday night, I was up to speed with the rest of the cast. The show was in great shape already, and I was proud to have fallen in line so seamlessly. By that Friday, opening night, everything was ready.

The cast was huge, close to 20 people in all, and so, in what would also become a trademark of shows which Bougie directed (no matter how small or large the cast) opening night was sold to the walls. From where I peeked out backstage it seemed like there were more people there than I had ever seen for any show at Trustus. It was very exciting.

My cue to enter came, and I walked out onstage. It must have been a shock for the audience to see me walk out. For the first 45 minutes there had only been African-Americans in white-face onstage, then, suddenly, here was an actual white man addressing the audience directly on an otherwise completely empty stage. I barreled into the newspeak verbiage that made up my introductory monologue, and everything was going fine.

About two-thirds of the way through my monologue was a line that was the cue for the townspeople who I was to interview to enter the stage. I was just about to the point of saying the line when my mind went completely blank. I came to the end of a sentence ... and the next one, which I had unfailingly remembered in all of the rehearsals leading up to this night, simply would not come. I was terrified, completely alone on the stage, no one there to cue me or to pick up with their next line in order to cover for my mistake, and about five cast members waiting just offstage for the line I was supposed to say that would cue them to enter. I looked over toward the box office and saw Bougie staring at me, which only made me feel more hopeless at being so completely blank.

I have no idea how long this went on. I was told that it was only for a few seconds, but it felt like days. The interviewees must have realized that I was floundering, because they began to enter, even though I hadn't delivered my cue line yet. Somehow this shook the frost off of my brain and the lines started to come out of me again. We finished the scene, the show, and I reluctantly took my bow with the rest of the ensemble, hung my head and ambled backstage.

I changed out of my costume, begged the stage

manager to bring me an open bottle of wine from the bar, and cowered backstage, trying to gather the courage it was going to take to go out into the house and face Bougie. I tucked my tail between my legs and wandered out. There were still a lot of people around, but I knew I had to say something to Bougie before I talked to anyone else. He was still standing near the box-office, talking to audience members as they were leaving. I saw my chance and approached him. The first thing he did was to put his arms around me in an embrace which I returned.

"Bougie," I stammered, "I am so sorry … I have no idea what happened to me up there…"

"It's okay…," he started.

"Bougie, I feel so bad for ruining your opening night."

"Alex," he said, smiling, "Don't worry about it."

"Really?"

"Really," he replied, still hugging me and smiling. "I'm sure the audience didn't notice that the white guy fucked up."

I never fucked my lines up again for the rest of the run.

Not that it matters now. The man from whom I asked mercy is gone. These and the many other memories I have of Bougie are, as Edwin Booth once described the greatest theatre performances ever given, "...masterpieces sculpted in ice." These things never end up the way we think they're going to.

I've struggled for months trying to figure out how to end this essay.

I had settled on a magical night almost a year after Bougie passed away. Darion McCloud's NiA Theatre Company was performing a show the proceeds from which would be used to make a donation to The Nickelodeon in order to put Bougie's name on a plaque attached to one of the new cinema's seats. It was Darion's idea; a way of commemorating the company's thanks to Bougie, and it was a good idea.

It wasn't until after the show on closing night, when we came out to greet the audience that we realized that Bougie's family was there. We all spent a long time talking to his mother, his sister, and the assorted relatives that were there, reminding them of the shows we'd worked on with Bougie, reminiscing, and laughing. At the end of the night, Darion and I and a couple of other company members walked Bougie's mother and sister to their car. They were so gracious, and so grateful that we had paid tribute to him.

It was utterly humbling, and that was going to be the end of what I wrote about Bougie.

But these things never end up the way we think they're going to.

Over Thanksgiving I finally got around to transferring an assortment of film footage from tape onto my more reliable hard drive. Two of the tapes I had forgotten existed. Their content consisted of the two acts of a play I directed in 2005 called *Topdog - Underdog*. I wilted at discovering them, because I consider that production to be the single best piece of theatre I've ever been a part of, and I didn't want this record to disprove me. I started transferring them and watching and, thankfully, I was reminded that I hadn't been wrong in my estimation.

But the thing that tied all this up happened about twelve or thirteen minutes into the first act. Something funny happened onstage, and the audience laughed ... and on top of that laughter, surrounding it, if possible, I heard Bougie's laugh.

Anybody who knew him will tell you that Bougie's laughter was unmistakable. When I was performing and I would hear his laughter in the audience from the stage, it was like having his arms around me, a place of utter safety and warmth and strength and genuine, unabashed love and caring. It felt like nothing could go wrong with the show whenever I heard his laugh.

And ever since he died, however present Bougie's spirit is in the stalls and the wings of all of the theatres in Columbia, it's his laughter that is missing still. Its absence is palpable, and it will echo forever in the memories of everyone who knew him; and we're lucky for it because his laughter, like Bougie himself, was singular.

About the Authors

Aïda Rogers is a Columbia writer and editor who has worked in newspapers, magazines, and television. She and Tim Driggers are coauthors of *Stop Where the Parking Lot's Full*, a guidebook to popular restaurants in South Carolina. She is the editor of *State of the Heart: South Carolina Writers on the Places They Love*, to be published by the University of South Carolina Press in May. She still dreams of a high-flying circus career.

Ed Madden is an associate professor of English at the University of South Carolina, where he is currently the interim director of the Women's & Gender Studies program. He is the author of three books of poetry: *Signals* (which won the SC Poetry Book Prize), *Prodigal: Variations*, and *Nest* (forthcoming 2014). His poems also appear in *Best New Poets 2007*, the Notre Dame anthology *The Book of Irish American Poetry*, and *Collective Brightness*.

Michael Miller graduated from the College of Charleston in 1976 with a degree in English. For the next six years, he was a surfer, tennis bum, bellhop, and shoe salesman. He eventually decided to get serious about writing and earned an MA in journalism from the University of South

Carolina in 1984. For almost 18 years, he was a reporter, features writer, and columnist for *The State* newspaper in Columbia. His work appeared in many newspapers, including the *Atlanta Constitution, Pittsburgh Post-Gazette*, and the *Detroit Free Press*, as well as in magazines such as *Billboard* and *Guitar World*. His biography of the rock band Hootie and the Blowfish was published by Summerhouse Press in 1997, and in 2007 he was a South Carolina Fiction Project winner. His first collection of short stories, *Lonesome Pines*, was published in 2008

Cynthia Boiter is a six time winner of the South Carolina Fiction Project, a two time winner of the Piccolo Fiction Open, a two time winner of the South Carolina Academy of Authors fellowship, and winner of the Porter Fleming Award for fiction. Her non-fiction work has appeared in national publications ranging from *Woman's Day and Family Circle* to *Southern Living*. She is the author of *Buttered Biscuits: Short Stories from the South* and the founder and editor-in-chief of *Jasper Magazine —The Word on Columbia Arts*.

Janna McMahan is the national bestselling author of the novels *Anonymity, Calling Home,* and *The Ocean Inside* and the novella *Decorations*. She has received a variety of awards for her short fiction including being selected as a finalist for the Flannery O'Connor Award. A widely published nonfiction writer, McMahan's personal essays and articles have appeared in a number of journals and magazines nationwide. Visit www.JannaMcMahan.com.

Jeffrey Day was arts writer at *The State* newspaper in Columbia for 19 years and prior to that arts and entertainment editor at *The Telegraph and News* in Macon, Ga. His work has been published in a variety of magazines and newspapers and art exhibition and art and music festival publications. He has been winner of a National Arts Journalism Fellowship and a National Endowment for the Arts Classical Music Fellowship.

Kristine Hartvigsen is a freelance writer based in Columbia, South Carolina, and the author of the poetry chapbook, *To the Wren Nesting*, published in 2012 by Muddy Ford Press. She serves as associate editor of *Jasper Magazine —The Word on Columbia Arts.* She also is a past editor of *South Carolina Business* and *Lake Murray-Columbia* magazines as well as a past contributing editor of *undefined* magazine. A self-taught poet and photographer, she was a finalist in the South Carolina Poetry Initiative's Single Poem Contest in 2010 and 2011.

A PhD student in 20th century American Literature at the University of South Carolina, *Kyle Petersen* got his start writing about music as a music director at the college radio station WUSC 90.5 FM, and has been writing about the South Carolina music scene ever since. Currently the music editor of the Columbia arts magazine *Jasper*, he also does frequent freelance work with Columbia's *Free Times* and the Carolinas-based *Shuffle* magazine, and continues to DJ a locals-oriented radio show each week.

August Krickel is a local writer, editor, and actor whose day jobs have often involved fundraising and public relations for universities and nonprofits. He has acted at Workshop, Town and Chapin Community Theatres, toured in professional productions of *The Road to Victory* and *The Wizard of Oz*, and directed at Act One Theatre. A former chair of the S.C. Commission on National and Community Service, Town Theatre board member, and two-term president of the Columbia Civitan Club, he has written for *Jasper, Briefs, Free Times, Classical Bulletin, Financial Outlook, Whoosh!,* and *Onstage Columbia*. Krickel is currently the theatre editor for *Jasper Magazine*.

Colena Corbett divides her time between working, studying, writing, and living around the borders of North and South Carolina. She has studied poetry at the Split Rock Arts Foundation at the University of Minnesota, the Hurston-Wright Foundation at American University, The Kentucky Women Writers' Conference, and the Callaloo Writers' Workshop at Brown University. Her work has been published in *Obsidian III, Folio Journal, Charlotte Observer, and The Chapel Hill News*.

Susan Lenz is a professional studio artist in Columbia, South Carolina. Her fiber artwork has been widely exhibited in international and national juried exhibitions and solo installations all over the country. She has been awarded fellowships to attend art residencies at the MacNamara Foundation, Studios Midwest, Hot Springs

National Park, and the Studios of Key West. Lenz's works have claimed three "Best of Show" awards in the fine craft competition, *Palmetto Hands:* first place ribbons in the 2011 National Heritage Quilt Show and the Living Heritage Museum in Athens, TN and the 2011 Wearable Arts Awards in Port Moody, British Columbia, and the Will's Creek Survey, Cumberland, MD. Represented by the Grovewood Gallery in Asheville, NC, she won the 2011 Niche Award for decorative fibers and is a finalist in the 2013 competition. Lenz is the *2012 Jasper Magazine Artist of the Year in Visual Arts.*

Cassie Premo Steele, Ph.D., is the author of eight books and two musical poetry albums on the themes of creativity, healing, spirituality, and living in balance with the natural world. She writes the monthly "Birthing the Mother Writer" column at www.LiteraryMama.com, named one of the Best 100 Websites for Writers by Writers' Digest, teaches monthly Earth Joy Writing classes at Saluda Shoals Park, and works as a writing and creativity coach with local and long-distance clients in academia and the arts from her Co-Creating Studio in Columbia. Her website is www.cassiepremosteele.com

Chad Henderson is a professional theatre director based out of Columbia, SC. He received a BA from The University of South Carolina where he majored in Advertising and minored in Theatre. On staff at Trustus Theatre as the Marketing Director, Henderson has directed shows at various venues including: Trustus Theatre, The

Studios of Key West, The Workshop Theatre of South Carolina, Theatre South Carolina, The Columbia Children's Theatre, Spartanburg Next Stage, and The Spartanburg Youth Theatre. His productions of *Dog Sees God: Confessions of a Teenage Blockhead* (2007) and *Avenue Q* (2012) were voted "Best Local Production" by readers of the *Free Times*. Henderson is the *2012 Jasper Magazine Artist of the Year in Theatre.*

Ray McManus is the author of two books of poetry: *Driving through the country before you are born* (USC Press 2008), and *Red Dirt Jesus* (Marick Press 2011). His poetry has appeared in many journals, most recently *Barely South*, *Pea River Review*, and *The Pinch.* Ray is an Assistant Professor of English in the Division of Arts and Letters at University of South Carolina Sumter, where he teaches creative writing, Irish literature, rhetoric, composition, and business writing.

Bonnie Boiter-Jolley is a professional ballet dancer with Columbia City Ballet. She has previously danced or studied with Spectrum Dance Theatre in Seattle, Wideman Davis Dance Company, Ballet Adriatico in Ascoli Piceno, Italy, the National Theatre Ballet in Prague, Jacob's Pillow in Massachusetts, American Ballet Theatre, and Alonzo King Lines Ballet. She is a graduate of the University of North Carolina School of the Arts in Dance and the University of South Carolina in Dance Performance and Political Science. She has written for the *Free Times* and is the dance editor for *Jasper Magazine.*

Robbie Robertson is a playwright and screenwriter and a graduate of the University of South Carolina and UCLA's professional program in screenwriting. Robertson's first play, *Mina Tonight*, was published by Samuel French Inc. in 1996 and has been consistently produced in regional theatres across the nation. He directed a staged version of two *Gilligan's Island* episodes at Trustus Theatre. His staged adaptation of the film *Satan in High Heels* received a staged reading by Trustus in 2012 and by the NYC based TOSOS Theatre Company in February 2013. Robertson also recently revived one of his first theatrical productions—the musical comedy The Twitty Triplets—as part of Trustus Theatre's New "Off Lady Street" series.

A South Carolina Writer's Workshop/Carrie McCray Literary Award winner, SC Fiction Project honoree, and Faulkner-Wisdom finalist, *James D. McCallister* has worked as a motion picture archivist, newspaper columnist, freelance journalist, small business owner, and author: fiction publications include stories in *Pearl*, *Sandlapper*, *Petigru Review*, and the *Saturday Evening Post*, as well as two novels, *King's Highway* (Red Letter Press, 2007) and *Fellow Traveler* (Muddy Ford Press, 2012); a third, *Dogs of Parson's Hollow*, is currently being shopped by the Corvisiero Literary Agency. McCallister teaches creative writing at Midlands Technical College and lives in West Columbia, SC, with his wife Jenn and their beloved brood of a dozen cats, muses all.

Alex Smith refuses to decide. He produces, acts, designs, and directs for the stage; acts in, writes, produces directs, shoots, scores, and edits film; is an accomplished and prolific visual artist; has published a book of his poetry; and (given the right circumstances) has been known to sing every now and then, and, even more rarely, to dance. Some of his recent endeavors include *An Evening with the Beats* at 701 Whaley for the 2012 What's Love Got To Do With It, participating in Columbia Open Studios for 701 CCA, and They're Wearing Bowlers, the completion of a 30 foot wide, 16 foot tall portrait of the characters from Samuel Beckett's *Waiting for Godot*.

About the Cover

Studio w/Figure Painting 2011 was created by artist Philip Mullen. An essay on Mullen by poet Cassie Premo Steele appears on page 115. He has had 15 New York solo exhibitions, most of which were with David Findlay Galleries. He and Steele like to create paintings and poetry that bypass the factual to get to the actual meaning.

About the Publisher

Muddy Ford Press, LLC is a family-owned publishing company dedicated to providing juried boutique publishing opportunities to, but not limited to, South Carolina writers, artists and poets.

About the Editor

Cynthia Boiter was born in Athens, Georgia and moved to Columbia, South Carolina first as an undergrad in 1977 and then, forever, in 1986. Her love for Columbia's arts and artists inspired both this book and the bi-monthly publication, *Jasper Magazine —The Word on Columbia Arts,* which she founded and edits. She is the author of *Buttered Biscuits: Short Fiction from the South* (Muddy Ford Press, 2012).